CHIRON: THE NEW PLANET IN YOUR HOROSCOPE, THE KEY TO YOUR QUEST

by

Richard Nolle

No part of this book may be reproduced or transmitted in any
form or by any means, electronic or mechanical, including
photocopying or recording, or by any information storage and
retrieval system, without written permission from the author
and publisher. Requests and inquiries may be mailed to:
American Federation of Astrologers, Inc., P.O. Box 22040,
Tempe, AZ 85285-2040.

First Printing 1983
Sixth Printing 1991
ISBN Number: 0-86690-236-8
Library of Congress Catalogue Card Number: 83-70810

Cover Design: Mary Martha Rader

Published by:
American Federation of Astrologers, Inc.
P.O. Box 22040, 6535 South Rural Road
Tempe, Arizona 85285-2040

Printed in the United States of America

TABLE OF CONTENTS

CHAPTER   **PAGE**

ACKNOWLEDGEMENTS

This book would not have been possible without the positive contributions of a number of friends and fellow astrologers. In particular, thanks are due to Julia Wagner, Editor-in-Chief of *Horoscope* magazine, whose interest in my early writings on Chiron (pronounced Ky-ron) helped sustain my work; to Zane Stein, Director of the Association for Studying Chiron, who has done so much to keep the Centaur Planet in the consciousness of the astrological community; to Ed Rieck, Gardiner James, Bill Hansen, Moon Moore, Michael Lutin and Erminie Lantero, for their helpful comments on many of the ideas expressed herein; and to the many fellow students of the cosmic art/science it was my pleasure to meet in connection with my Chiron lectures at the Planet Earth Book Center in Ft. Myers, Florida, the Astrological Research Guild at Orlando, Florida and the 1982 American Federation of Astrologers' convention in Chicago — although too numerous to be recognized individually, these many fine people know who they are, and they deserve recognition for the probing questions that prodded me to rewrite portions of this book.

In addition, I wish to acknowledge the indirect contributions of a number of people who have helped blaze a trail for the Centaur Planet in astrology, without whom this book would have been impossible. Thanks to James Neely, Eric Tarkington, Mark Pottenger, Michael Campbell, Tony Joseph and Malcolm Dean, for publishing their *Ephemeris of Chiron* (which gives Chiron positions for the years 1686 to 2000); and to Neil Michelsen, for including monthly Chiron positions in *The American Ephemeris for the 20th Century*. These excellent ephemerides enable astrologers everywhere to study Chiron's significance in their own natal horoscopes, as well as in the birth charts of friends, clients, countries, cities, events, etc.

Last but certainly not least, I am grateful for the patience and encouragement of Maria and Dylan, who allowed me the solitude necessary to complete this work; and of course this entire project would never have seen the light of day without the interest and support of the American Federation of Astrologers and in particular Bob and Sara Cooper.

Thank you one and all!

Richard Nolle
Orlando, Florida
March 9, 1983

INTRODUCTION

The introduction to a book, it seems to me, really ought to serve as a set of user instructions. It ought to tell for whom the book is written, and why, and how the reader might best set about getting the most out of the book. All these things should be made clear from the outset, as a courtesy to the reader no less than out of respect for the thousands of trees who give their lives for the sake of books. True, when the book is printed it's already too late for the trees. But if the book falls into the right hands, then at least the trees died for something! Therefore, Dear Reader, I offer this brief introduction in the hope it will enable you to determine if this is the right book for you.

This book is written for astrologers and their students. That's saying a lot! There are thousands of practicing astrologers in the United States, and millions of Americans have studied astrology at least to the point of learning their sun sign. For all our varying levels of study and experience, every one of us is at heart a student of the cosmic art/science. We are all in our own way in search of the answers to life's riddles, and that is precisely what astrology is for. From the professional with many years' experience as a teacher, lecturer, writer or counselor, to the person who has just discovered that he or she has a thing called a "Sign", we are students for life. There are always new realities to be discovered, new questions to be asked, old answers to be re-examined.

Casual students of astrology, it is safe to say, are not in a position to fully appreciate this book. By casual students, I mean those who have not yet developed the capacity to calculate and interpret a horoscope. Certainly there can be no one who can realistically lay claim to having fully mastered this capacity. It's something you grow into, and if you do it right, you never stop growing. If you already know how to compute and interpret a chart, you've come to the right place. If not, please consult the selected bibliography, which details the references and primers you'll need to get started. Meanwhile please bear in mind that you need be no more than a casual student of astrology to use and understand the chapter on Chiron signs (Chapter 6) — all it takes is your birthdate (see Appendix I). Students could start studying astrology any number of ways, but most of us get our feet wet with our own natal horoscope. There is a reason for this, a very good one in fact. The purpose of astrology is to fulfill the Socratic maxim, "Know Thyself". Unless you can discover the truth in your own horoscope, all others (charts and truths) will be inaccessible. Serious students of astrology, by definition, already have a copy of their own birth chart. If the chart does not include the recently-discovered Minor Planet Chiron, they should be able to calculate Chiron's position and incorporate it into the horoscope. The selected bibliography lists all the references needed to facilitate this computation.

Many very good students of astrology for one reason or another prefer not to get involved in the mathematical busy-work of chart calculation. They may have the training and intuitive knack required to excel in delineating the chart, but they just don't enjoy doing the math. Many casual students as well, even if they had the proper training, would just as soon avoid calculations altogether. For the benefit of readers who fall in either category, Appendix II furnishes full information on a low-cost, high-quality chart computing service that specializes in natal horoscopes which include Chiron.

This book is written from the perspective of a deep personal conviction that the Minor Planet Chiron is in many respects the key to understanding one's natal horoscope. No one can number the myriad functions contained in a single horoscope. Every one of them — every Planet, sign, house, aspect, element, quality, planetary pattern, Part, Node or what-have-you — is crucial; each contributes to the whole in which it subsists. But in this whole vast universe of astrological functions, there is only one that is archetypally linked to the teaching and learning of astrology. That one and only function is Chiron.

I do not mean to make the claim that one's understanding of astrology is worthless without Chiron — only that it is incomplete. Yet even with the addition of Chiron, no one can be said to have a final and complete grasp of the cosmic art/science. There are no gurus, only chelas; no masters, only students. This too is something Chiron has to teach us.

Many of us, early in our careers as students, have puzzled over the astrological dilemma posed by the Planet Pluto. How did astrologers manage at all before 1930, when Pluto was discovered? After it became known, how did this knowledge change the teaching and practice of astrology? All who have pondered these and like questions realize that the discovery of a new Planet has a momentous revitalizing effect on the Hermetic Discipline. So it is with Chiron. How does one attempt the incredible feat of incorporating a new Planet into one's astrological vocabulary? On a practical level, a good place to start is through coming to know the archetypal nature of the Planet itself. In addition it is helpful to consider delineations (which are based on the Planetary archetype) of the Planet in relation to the signs, houses and aspects. There are worlds of refinement beyond these, to be sure, including information drawn from individual case histories and mass studies. This book aims to acquaint you with all these topics.

What is the highest and best use of this book? That is of course a question which must ultimately be answered by the student on his or her own terms. My objective is to acquaint you with the meaning and expression of Chiron as I have come to know him, in the hope that you will assimilate these ideas, bring them to life in your own consciousness, and grow from there. It's quite all right to pick up a book looking for answers, but it's a terrible waste of time and energy if, after reading the book, you do not have more questions than you did when you started. Chiron is a most dynamic Planetary archetype. He is the Quest Guide, the Initiator. I have no doubt that you will discover him personally if only you will use this book as a springboard for your own Hermetic quest.

How do you get started? The lesson plan is really very simple. Study Chiron's archetypal meaning — meditate on it. Search for correspondences in your own life and in your own horoscope. Consider the delineations of Chiron's expression in terms of house, sign, aspect, etc. For Heaven's sake, do not mistake these delineations for anything other than what they are — mere outlines, which make real sense only when fleshed out by the light of your own experience.

In his own peculiar and fascinating way, Chiron is the most mystical of all the Planets. Even foggy Neptune seems a bit out of his depth in the presence of the wily old Centaur. I do not for a moment mean to suggest that one must become a full-blown mystic to understand Chiron. His mysticism is the most mystical of all — the practical kind. The Chironian quest has always a practical object in mind, but at the same time it always takes place as a necessary element in the fulfillment of one's spiritual destiny. Do I seem to contradict myself? If so, it is only because the essence of Chiron itself is dialectical, a polarized union of opposites.

It is in regard to the mystical nature of Chiron, I suspect, that some of my fellow astrologers may take issue with what I have to say. Astrology in recent years has seemed to struggle against its own mystical heritage, in an effort to gain respectability in an increasingly scientific and technical world. I too have done my share of number-crunching emphirical research, even on the subject of Chiron. In the process I have come to see confirmed what my intuition told me all along; namely that numbers and computers deserve each other, but that people deserve something else — certainly not anything less, mind you (computers are wonderful tools), but something more. Therefore I make no apology for including the chapter entitled "Not the Last Chapter", as I have no doubt that to introduce the Centaur without the benefit of the Guide meditation would be to undermine the very meaning of Chiron.

Chiron is a key, Dear Reader. What doors this key may open in your life, neither you nor I can guess at this moment. But I do feel certain, at the very least, that in time Chiron will reveal to you a new kind of astrology, a participatory psychodrama of personal transmutation. And I trust you will come to see, as have I, that this process is nothing less than the Cosmic Alchemy which is the very essence of astrology.

CHAPTER 1

AN ASTRONOMICAL DISCOVERY

It happened around 10:00 A.M. (Pacific Standard Time) on November 1, 1977, at Pasadena, California. Using a Blink Microscope, astronomer Charles Kowal of the Hale Observatory was scanning a set of photographic plates taken by the 48-inch telescope at Mt. Palomar some two weeks earlier (on the night of October 18 and 19, to be specific). The Blink Microscope is a tool used by astronomers to detect extremely faint and apparently slow-moving objects in the heavens. It works rather like an animated cartoon. Two photos are rapidly alternated to produce the illusion of motion. Stationary objects remain stationary when the two plates are alternated, but a moving object shows up as such. When he ran the plates of October 18 and 19, Kowal discovered just such a moving object. It was faint and remote, the dancing point of light that moved against its starry backdrop.

To the ancient Greeks, everything in the heavens was a star — but some stars were different. There were falling stars (meteors), hairy stars (comets) and wandering stars (Planets), in addition to the distant stellar objects we normally think of in connection with the word star. Charles Kowal knew that what he had discovered was not a star because it moved from one night to the next. Stars, even though they hurtle along at tremendous velocities, are so distant from Earth that they show no apparent motion relative to each other even over periods of many centuries.

Uncertain at first exactly what he had discovered, Kowal suspected it was either a comet or a Minor Planet. But a comet this large? The object was a hundred times the size of a typical comet nucleus! Perhaps it was a Minor Planet, an errant asteroid. The asteroids are Minor Planets in orbit around the Sun, generally in the space between Mars and Jupiter. Calculation of the newfound object's path through space revealed that it held to an orbit lying for

1

the most part between the Planets Saturn and Uranus — an unlikely niche for an asteroid. To be sure, there are a number of Minor Planets (such as those belonging to the Amor class of objects) that do not confine themselves to the classical Asteroid Belt between Mars and Jupiter. But no such object had ever been discovered with an orbit as far-flung as this one! Kowal provisionally named his new find, appropriately enough, Object Kowal. The name was soon changed to Chiron (in honor of the mythical Chief Centaur), and it has since stuck. We now know that Chiron is indeed a Minor Planet, albeit a most unusual one. As Minor Planets go, Chiron is rather large, with an estimated diameter something on the order of 150 to 650 kilometers (about 100 to 400 miles). Compare the larger estimate to Ceres, which at 1,000 kilometers in diameter is the biggest of the classical asteroids. If the larger estimate of Chiron's size proves correct, Ceres is the only denizen of the Asteroid Belt to surpass Chiron in size. Even if the smaller estimate turns out to be nearer to the truth, only about fifteen of the more than 50,000 asteroids are larger than Chiron. (All the Minor Planets are small in comparison to the Earth — in fact the total mass of all the asteroids taken together is estimated to be less than one-tenth of one percent the mass of Earth).

Just what is a Minor Planet, exactly? For the purposes of this discussion, let us define a Minor Planet as a natural satellite of the Sun characterized by smaller mass and size than the known Major Planets. The Major Planets, for our purposes, are Mercury, Venus, Earth, Mars, Jupiter, Saturn, Uranus, Neptune and Pluto. (Note: Astronomers use the term Major Planet to mean the four giants of the Planetary family — Jupiter, Saturn, Uranus and Neptune. We're using the term in a special sense here, which accounts for the divergence from normal astronomical practice. It should also be noted, incidentally, that astronomers and astrologers alike speculate there may be an undiscovered Major Planet outside the orbits of Neptune and Pluto.) In terms of these distinctions, all the bodies comprising the Asteroid Belt are Minor Planets, as are a number of eccentric asteroids which have been discovered in orbits outside the traditional Asteroid Belt.

How small must a solar satellite be to qualify as a Minor Planet? Well, think of tiny Mercury, only some 4,900 kilometers (about 3,100 miles) in diameter. Our own Earth, with an equatorial diameter of 12,756 kilometers (7,296 miles), is more than twice Mercury's size. The only Major Planet thought to be smaller than Mercury is faraway Pluto. Estimates for Pluto vary greatly, ranging anywhere from 2,900 kilometers (about 1,800 miles) to 4,800

2

kilometers (roughly 3,000 miles) in diameter — the latest estimates tend toward the smaller end of the spectrum. Compared to even the smallest of the Major Planets, Chiron is very small indeed, even though it is relatively large as Minor Planets go. Chiron has a number of notable distinctions besides its size. For one thing, this Minor Planet has a most eccentric orbit. Think of it this way: assign every Planet a number corresponding to the eccentricity of its orbit, and let the numbers range from zero to one. Those Planets with the most nearly circular orbits will have numbers close to zero. Those with the least circular orbits will have numbers greater than zero, but less than one. An object not orbiting the Sun at all, but passing through the solar system on an open-ended path, would have the highest possible rating; namely one. Where does Chiron fit in these terms? Just barely, that's where! With an eccentricity factor of 0.0068, Venus has the most nearly circular orbit of any Major Planet. Until Pluto's discovery in 1930, the most eccentric Major Planet was Mercury, whose elliptical orbit equates to an eccentricity factor of 0.2056. Pluto then took the honors for most elliptical path, with a rating of 0.2482. Then along comes Chiron, with a factor of 0.3786! What this means is that Chiron's orbit is some fifty percent more eccentric than even the most errant Major Planet's path.

Chiron's orbital oddities do not end with this rather extreme elliptical nature. Chiron also shares a certain transorbital wanderlust with Pluto. Pluto, as most of us were taught in school, is the outermost known Planet. But as often happens, what we're taught in school turns out to be something less than the whole truth. The fact of the matter is that Pluto's eccentric orbit carries this small Planet inside the orbit of Neptune once every 248 years. When this happens, Neptune — not Pluto — is the outermost known Planet. (Indeed, this is exactly what took place on December 11, 1978, when Pluto moved inside Neptune's orbit. Not until March 14, 1999, will Pluto once more swing outside Neptune's path.)

When discovered, Chiron lay in the orbital niche between Saturn and Uranus, two of our solar system's ringed giants. However, calculation of Chiron's path reveals that at perihelion (closest approach to the Sun) this Minor Planet moves inside the orbit of Saturn. And when Chiron reaches aphelion (maximum distance from the Sun), it is actually farther from Sol than is Uranus when Uranus is at perihelion. But because Chiron does not reach aphelion in the same part of Uranus' orbit where the latter comes to perihelion, Chiron does not cross over Uranus' orbit as it does Saturn's.

Orbital oddities of this order have led astronomers to daring speculations about both Pluto and Chiron. Each is suspected of being a cosmic renegade. Pluto, it is said, may be an escaped moon of Neptune. Chiron's genesis may be even more fantastic. According to Dr. Brian Marsden of the Smithsonian Center for Astrophysics, Chiron might not even be native to our solar system, but instead a wandering chunk of matter captured from out of the depths of interstellar space. And the capture could even prove to be only temporary, for according to Dr. Marsden's calculations, Chiron's orbit is unstable enough that it may someday (in the far distant future!) be cast out of our solar system back into the boundless realm whence it came.

Given its oddball orbit, you may wonder how Chiron manages to avoid colliding with Saturn. For that matter, what keeps Pluto from smashing into Neptune? After all in each case we have a set of orbits that intersect — how can that mean anything but catastrophe on a cosmic scale? The answer in both cases is the same, and it reveals another peculiarity these two cosmic renegades Pluto and Chiron have in common. For starters, you must understand that the zodiac of astrology is defined as the apparent path of the Sun as viewed from a geocentric (i.e. Earth-centered) perspective. From a heliocentric (i.e. Sun-centered) viewpoint, this path is equivalent to Earth's orbit. Astronomers and astrologers alike call this path the ecliptic — the plane of Earth's orbit in space. No other Planet's orbital plane exactly matches the plane of the ecliptic. From Mercury out to Neptune (or Pluto, depending on when you happen to be reading this!), all the Planets' orbits are inclined at an angle to the ecliptic.

What has the ecliptic to do with Chiron and Pluto avoiding collisions with their neighbors in space? These two Planets, you see, follow orbits that are rather steeply inclined to the plane of the ecliptic. Other than Pluto, whose inclination to the ecliptic is the most radical of any Major Planet, no Major Planet but Mercury follows an orbit more steeply inclined to the ecliptic than Chiron. Pluto's inclination is 17 degrees and 8 minutes. Mercury's is 7 degrees even. Chiron's is only slightly less than that, at 6 degrees and 55 minutes. No other Major Planet's angle of inclination is even half as steep as Chiron's! These varying degrees of inclination to the ecliptic plane are the reason Neptune and Pluto do not collide, nor Saturn and Chiron. At the points where their orbits do cross, one Planet passes above the other, and catastrophe is averted.

What else is known about Chiron, astronomically speaking? Well, its orbital period is about 50 years, give or take a few months. At perihelion (the last time was in August 1945 — the next time will be in February, 1996), Chiron is about 1,273,000,000 kilometers (791,000,000 miles) from the Sun. At aphelion (the last time was in December, 1970), Chiron is some 2,826,000,000 kilometers (1,756,000,000 miles) distant from Sol. It is a body without sufficient mass to hold an atmosphere, and apparently has no satellites in orbit around it. The length of Chiron's day remains unknown at this point — no one can tell how long this little orb takes to turn about its own axis. That's about all the astronomers can tell us about the Centaur Planet.

You may wonder why astronomers took so long to discover Chiron. Part of the answer may be that no one really expected to find anything of consequence in the orbital niche Chiron occupies, between Saturn and Uranus. Uranus, like Chiron, was found quite by accident. The real wonder about Uranus is that it had to wait for the invention of the telescope to be discovered, as this Planet at its brightest is visible (albeit just barely) to the naked eye. But Neptune (discovered in 1846) and Pluto (discovered in 1930) were both eventually found because someone expected them to be there. Based on observed anomalies in the orbits of known Planets and comets, astronomers reasoned that something had to be out there to cause these anomalies. They looked where their calculations told them to look, and (Eureka!) they found what they were looking for.

Likewise the asteroids (Ceres, the first to be discovered, was sighted in 1801) were found because someone expected to find something orbiting between Mars and Jupiter. As early as 1596, Johannes Kepler speculated that "between Jupiter and Mars there must be a Planet." A couple hundred years or so later, Johann Titius and Johann Bode took up Kepler's idea and promoted it in a systematic way. These two had noticed what appeared to be an orderly spacing of Planetary distances from the Sun. The theory that there is a regular progression of Planetary orbits came to be known as Bode's Law. The only problem with Bode's Law was the space between Jupiter and Mars — the theory called for a Planet in this space, and yet none could be found. With the discovery of the Minor Planet Ceres, which happened to be right where Bode's Law said it should be, the intuitions and deductions of Kepler, Titius and Bode seemed vindicated. In any case, the important point for our purposes is that each of these discoveries was anticipated — someone thought something should be out there, and someone with a telescope eventually found it.

Chiron's discovery, in contrast, was strictly serendipitous — a happy accident. No astronomer expected to find a Planet were Chiron was found, and consequently no one was specifically search-

5

ing for one. (Charles Kowal, it turns out, was actually looking for Trojan-class asteroids and stray comets when, quite by accident, he discovered Chiron — serendipity indeed!) Ironically, Chiron was actually seen and photographed long before it was officially discovered. There are some thirty telescopic photos of Chiron known to have been taken prior to its announced discovery, dating back as far as April 24, 1895. One plate taken in 1941 even had Chiron's dancing point of light circled, but for reasons unknown to us this was never followed up. So why did we have to wait until 1977 for the happy news? The obvious practical answer, it seems to me, is that a quirk of human nature often prevents us from recognizing something unless we first anticipate it. The obvious metaphysical answer is, quite simply, that the time was not yet ripe prior to 1977. Whatever the reason, the irony of Chiron's discovery takes on an especially curious irony when you realize that, while astronomers did not anticipate Chiron, astrologers did.

The first astrologer to anticipate the discovery of the Minor Planet we know as Chiron appears to have been Maurice Wemyss (pseudonym for Duncan McNaughton) of Scotland. Around 1935 Wemyss' *The Wheel of Life, Vol. 4* was published, telling of a hypothetical Planet in orbit between Saturn and Uranus, having an orbital period of 45 years. Wemyss named this Planet Jason — a significant point because in Greek mythology Jason was a hero whose mentor and foster-father was none other than Chiron! The eminent astrologer Dane Rudhyar also seems to have foreseen Chiron in his book *The Astrology of Personality*, published in 1936. In this book, Rudhyar speaks of what he calls a "Higher Moon" symbolically linking Uranus and the Sun, and tells of a 56-year period for this body which turned out to be not too far from Chiron's actual 50.682 year mean orbital cycle. Last but certainly not least, the noted American astrologer Charles Jayne, in the Winter-Spring 1961 issue of his magazine *In Search*, told of a hypothetical Planet having an orbital period of 50 years ("plus or minus two years") and penetrating the orbit of Saturn. This Planet, Jayne ventured to guess, would be discovered around 1975!

The story of the Minor Planet Chiron's relationship to humanity began, in an objective sense at least, with its discovery in 1977. However important the actual astronomical discovery may be, it is no less important to realize that Chiron was anticipated by astrologers long before it entered the awareness of astronomers. A full understanding of the Centaur Planet requires a synthesis of its astronomical characteristics, to be sure. But it is also necessary to apprehend the mythical and historical legacy of Chiron, for these contribute to our understanding as well. We have so far touched on only one of these categories. As we proceed in subsequent chapters, keep in mind what has been presented up to this point, for it holds an important key to the ultimate astrological assimilation of Chiron's significance for humankind.

CHAPTER 2

TALE OF THE CENTAUR CHIEF

A myth, we are commonly told, is merely a fanciful story. There was a time (it ended, by and large, around the 5th Century B.C.E.), when myth was known for what it really is — not a fanciful tale, but a revelation. In our own highly technological era we have mostly forgotten what cannot be seen and quantified directly or through instruments, and so we tend to disparage mythology. Still there remain some who recognize unseen realities, psychic archetypes that shape our every experience and perception. In fact there is inside each of us a magical being who knows and responds to the verities of myth.

A myth is not created by humankind. Rather, the reverse is true — it is we who are created by myth. Cut off from our mythical heritage by our culture, as so many of us are today, we are divorced from our own magical potential. Is it any wonder that science and technology arose when myth ceased to hold its power over human endeavor, and that in consequence we are faced with a dehumanized world at best — perhaps even with the end of the world as far as human beings are concerned? The scientist may scoff, the technologist may deny it, but the human heart knows it is true.

Myth foretold its own decline, in the story of Prometheus. It was Prometheus, you will recall, who defied the gods and brought fire (technology) to human beings. The gods knew what Prometheus could only guess; that the fire he had delivered into human hands spelled the dawn of a new world order in which the gods would be driven away from the human fold. Driven away, mind you — not forgotten, and certainly not destroyed. For the gods live inside us and all around us, although we no longer pay them homage in any conscious, purposeful way. And yet we are only partly conscious, we use only a tiny fraction of our mental capacity in purposeful thought and action. The better part of us, as it always has, continues to live in that mythical realm.

Astrology and myth go hand-in-hand, at once partaking of the same magical order of reality. All the Planets in your horoscope are named for mythical gods of old — and not merely by historical accident did this come to pass. These Planetary gods correspond to psychic potentialities (psychological functions, if you will) that go to make up your very being. They are who they are not because we or our ancestors decided these things. Rather we are who we are because of them; it is we who are created in their image.

Take Chiron, for instance. One who is mired in the delusion of matter (call it objectivity, empiricism or what-you-will) might argue that the Minor Planet we know as Chiron would be the same no matter what Charles Kowal had decided to name his discovery. But I tell you truly that Kowal was fated to tap into the archetype of Chiron, thus bringing to the forefront of human consciousness all the magical energy contained in the legends of the Centaur Chief.

The first gods were elementals and animals, quite different from the later humanlike gods of the Olympian order. The zodiac of astrology preserves many of the old divinities, with their alien forms. Consider the Ram, the Bull, the Crab, the Lion, the Scorpion, the Sea-Goat and the Fishes — all the so-called bestial signs are vestiges of the old gods. The remaining signs, save only one, belong to the order of humanlike gods — the Twins, the Virgins, the Scales (called humane by Ptolemy, often symbolized by a woman holding a balance) and the Water-Bearer. The one exception to this zodiacal dichotomy is the Centaur, Sagittarius. Half-human, half-bestial, this sign alone represents an intermediary form between the old and the new gods.

The Centaur of Sagittarius is none other than Chiron, according to most authorities, although some associate Chiron with the constellation Centaurus. Nearly everyone is familiar with the figure of the Centaur; a creature having the body and limbs of a horse, together with the torso, arms and head of a human being. Human from the waist up and animal below, the race of Centaurs had a formidable reputation in the ancient world. It is said that they were violent hedonists, savage and lusty beyond compare — especially when they were drunk, which was as often as they could arrange it. Chiron alone, myth tells us, was the exception. He was universally regarded as kind, wise, noble and just.

Chiron's geneology is a blend of gods old and new. His grandfather was Uranus, the Sky, and his grandmother was Gaea, the Earth — both gods of the primeval elemental order. The children of

9

Uranus and Gaea were mostly monsters, although some (the Titans) were human in appearance. Uranus oppressed and imprisoned all his sons. However one of the Titans, Saturn by name, escaped and overthrew his father. Saturn then became ruler of Earth and Sky, together with his wife Rhea. It was not a union hallowed by fidelity, for old Saturn had a roving eye.

It happened one day that Saturn took a fancy to Philyra, a daughter of his brother Oceanus. As any astrologer can tell you, Saturn gets what Saturn wants, sooner or later (usually later). In time, Saturn had his way with Philyra. Faithful he was not, but Saturn was the very soul of discretion. He took the form of a stallion before he bedded down with his niece, in order to conceal his affair from Rhea. As a result, the myth says, the issue of his illicit union turned out to be the first of the Centaurs, half-horse, half-human. They named him Chiron.

Saturn had other offspring as well, legitimate children borne by Rhea. These he promptly ate, fearing they might grow up to treat him as he had treated his own father. However Rhea deceived Saturn when their son Jupiter was born. She hid the baby, and when Saturn demanded he be given the child to eat, she handed over a rock wrapped in swaddling clothes. Thus spared by a ruse, Jupiter grew up to overthrow his father, and thereafter ruled supreme over Earth and Sky.

Jupiter and Chiron were half-brothers, and together they shared a sanctuary in the cave where Chiron was born. Located on Mt. Pelion, the cave was called the Chironian. Jupiter, as you might expect, insisted on having the choice southern exposure, so Chiron was left with the north side of the cave. Thus it came to pass that Jupiter held sway over the diurnal (day-side) portion of the Chironian, and Chiron himself had dominion over the nocturnal (night-side) part of the sanctuary.

Chiron was the first of the race of Centaurs, and was acknowledged as chief among them. His fellow Centuars were, as he, unions of the animal and the human. While in them the worst part of the animal nature was dominant, in Chiron the best of the human spirit found full expression. He was acknowledged by mortals and immortals alike as "the wisest of all things beneath the sky." As perfect a balance of animal and human nature as ever lived, Chiron was attuned to the secrets of both instinct and intellect.

Myth tells us little of Chiron's personal life. He was married to the Naiad Charicles, one of the water goddesses who dwelt in brooks, fountains and streams. Their only offspring was a daughter, Thea the Prophetess. Thea means shining, a name sometimes given to the Moon. In view of Thea's psychic renown, it is a curious coincidence that her name would be translatable as the title of Stephen King's classic psychic horror novel, *The Shining*. Coincidence or not ("It'll shine when it shines!"), it is worthy of note that Thea foretold that her father would oneday long to give up his immortality.

The Chief Centaur lived most of his life in the cave atop Mt. Pelion. To the Chironian came, as children, many of the great heroes celebrated in Greek myth. Chiron became both foster parent and teacher to these child heroes. As he raised them up, the Centaur Chief inculcated in his wards the values and knowledge they would later need to pursue their epic quests. He sought to make each of his students a man for all seasons, striving to make each a whole man in every sense of the world. The arts of music, astrology, surgery, herbal medicine, hunting, riding and combat were part of the curricula under Chiron. However the Centaur recognized that he alone, being an immortal, could excel in all these fields, and so he always encouraged those of his students whose talents were not so universal.

To Achilles, Jason, Actaeon, Peleus and Hercules, he taught the skills of war, hunting and riding. To Orpheus and Aristaeus, he imparted a love and talent for music. To Achilles and Asclepius, Chiron gave the arts of surgery and herbal medicine; Jason too excelled in the latter discipline. And to Hercules and Asclepius, Chiron taught the cosmic art/science, astrology. The Centaur Chief was renowned as a master of all these disciplines, but his real reputation was not so much that of a practitioner as it was that of a teacher.

Chiron's pupils came to him not out of idle curiousity, but in order to fulfill their destiny. Consider Jason, one of the Centaur Chief's most illustrious students. Long before his birth, the workings of destiny set into motion the events that would lead to Jason's legendary voyage on the good ship Argo, in search of the Golden Fleece. It all began with Athamas, King of the Minuans, whose wife Nephele bore him a son and a daughter, Phrixus and Helle, respectively. After a time Athamas grew tired of his wife, had her put away, and then married the wicked Princess Ino. Jealous of her two stepchildren, fearful that they might inherit the throne she coveted for her own line, Ino plotted against Phrixus and Helle.

When a famine came on the land, Ino saw her chance. She demanded that Phrixus and Helle be sacrificed to appease the gods. The Minuan people, crazed by fear and starvation, agreed with Ino, and the two innocents were bound on an altar. As the priest's knife was poised ready to slash them, a miraculous Golden Ram swooped down out of the clouds and carried the two children away. Flying high over land and sea, the Ram was passing over the straits of the

Thracian Chersonese when Helle fell off. She plunged to her death in those narrow straits, everafter known as Hellespont in remembrance of her. Phrixus managed to hold on, and at last the Golden Ram set him down at Colchis, where Aietes was king. There Phrixus was well received, and won the hand of Aietes' daughter Chalchiope in marriage. In appreciation for his miraculous delivery and sudden good fortune, Phrixus sacrificed the Golden Ram to the gods. He gave the Ram's Golden Fleece to Aietes, who nailed it to a beech tree in the grove sacred to Mars.

Time passed, Phrixus died and was buried. But his spirit had no rest so far from his native land. The ghost of Phrixus visited the Minuan people in their sleep, begging them to return the Golden Fleece to the Minuan homeland, and thereby grant peace to Phrixus' spirit. Meanwhile Phrixus' father and cruel stepmother had died, and the Minuans were ruled by Aeson, a cousin to Phrixus. Unfortunately Aeson had a wicked stepbrother, Pelias by name, who usurped the throne and exiled the house of Aeson. Fleeing from Pelias, Aeson led his little son Jason by the hand toward Pelion, legendary home of the wise and just Chiron. Aeson left Jason in Chiron's care, beseeching the Centaur to train the boy among the sons of heroes, "that he may avenge his father's house."

To make a long story short, Jason passed ten years under Chiron's tutelage, alongside other boys who would grow up to be the stuff of legends. There was Aeneas, the founder of Rome, and Hercules, whose fame requires no explanation; also Asclepius the Healer and Peleus, the father of Achilles. Jason grew up strong, brave and cunning, but also wise — for the Centaur taught his wards the holistic virtues. He learned to fight and hunt, to play the lyre and to heal all wounds and sickness with medicinal herbs. Perhaps most important, he took to heart Chiron's injunction to treat everyone with kindness, and to honor a pledge given in good faith no matter what the consequence.

When the time came, Jason, with the assistance of many of Chiron's former pupils (among them Hercules, Peleus and Orpheus), built the great ship Argo. With a crew of fifty heroes, Jason and the Argonauts set sail for Colchis, fought for and won the Golden Fleece. After an odyssey of incredible adventures and tribulations, Jason at last returned the Fleece to his homeland, set the soul of his ancestor Phrixus to rest, and was made king of the Minuans.

The legend of Jason and the Argonauts is in many respects fundamental to the Chiron myth, a point to which we shall return later. But there are others as well that serve to illustrate the archetypal function of the Centaur Chief. Consider Orpheus, the legendary musician who learned his art at least in part from Chiron, and whose lyre and song were said to have irresistable power over all things animate and inanimate. Orpheus fell in love with Eurydice, so the story goes, and she responded in kind. At their wedding feast, Eurydice was walking in a meadow with her bridesmaids when a viper bit her.

Eurydice died from the venom, and Orpheus was overcome with grief. He made his way to the Underworld, and played a song for Pluto, pleading for Eurydice's release. Pluto fell under the spell of Orpheus' magical lyrics, and granted his request — with one condition. Eurydice would be allowed to follow Orpheus back to the land of mortals, but if he looked back at her before they both passed out of that realm of darkness, she would be snatched back to Hades and held there forever. So the two were allowed to leave Pluto's chamber, and began climbing the upward path that leads to the living world. But at the last instant, just as he stepped out into the light, Orpheus looked back to make sure Eurydice was still behind him. When he turned to look, he saw to his horror that Eurydice was still half in shadow, still one foot in Pluto's domain. In the blink of an eye she vanished, and Orpheus never saw her again until the day death closed his eyes.

Asclepius, the most celebrated healer in mythology, studied with Jason at the Chironian. It was said that Asclepius was the son of Apollo and the mortal maiden Coronis. Their union was not a happy one, for Coronis preferred the affections of a mortal over Apollo. Enraged, Apollo had Coronis killed. As her body lay on the funeral pyre, Apollo was overcome with grief over what he had done. The god rushed into the flames at the last moment and delivered his unborn son from Coronis' womb. Apollo took the baby, whom he named Asclepius, to the Chironian, and prevailed upon the Centaur Chief to raise the child.

Gentler in disposition than his classmates, Asclepius was in many ways Chiron's favorite pupil and foster child. While Hercules and the others excelled in feats of strength, Asclepius devoted his time to mastering the art of healing. He was familiar with all manner of medicinal herbs, adept at surgery, and blessed with a gift for psychic diagnosis and healing: All these things he learned at Chiron's feet. Astrology too became in the hands of Asclepius a powerful healing tool. He learned the correspondence between celestial configurations and the parts of the body, and the relationship between lunar phases and surgery.

When he had grown, Asclepius' reputation as a healer spread far and wide. It was said there was nothing he could not cure. Eventually it came to pass that Asclepius went so far as to raise Hippolytus from the dead. For this, Jupiter struck the physician down with a thunderbolt, for he would allow no mortal to have such power. And yet, hundreds of years after his death, sufferers came from all over Greece to temples that were dedicated to the memory of Asclepius. In these temples they would pray and sacrifice, then go to sleep. As they slept, inspired dreams came to them, prescribing the cures required to set the patient back on the road to recovery. Even in death, Asclepius retained his healing touch.

Chiron is remembered not only for his students, even though they were the greatest heroes of Greek myth. Equally important to the legend of the Centaur Chief were the events set into motion, some say, at the wedding of Hippodamia to Hercules' friend Pirithous. There were Centaurs at the wedding, Chiron among them. In the course of the festivities his fellow Centaurs proceeded to get drunk, whereupon they began forcing their affections on the women present. A great fight ensued, as ordinary mortals and celebrated heroes clashed with the Centaurs in deadly combat. At last, with Hercules' help, the Centaurs were routed.

When it was over, Chiron was the only Centaur left, for he was the only one who had not been caught up in the drinking and fighting. The Chief Centaur picked up one of Hercules' poison arrows, meaning to return it to his friend and student. But the arrow slipped out of the Centaur's fingers, and dropped by chance on his foot. Wounded by a powerful venom he himself had taught Hercules to make, the Centaur could not cure his poisoned flesh. Burning with pain and yet an immortal, Chiron faced an eternal agony and he knew it. To end his suffering, the Centaur willingly gave up his immortality to Prometheus[1] . Some say it was because Chiron had grown tired of everlasting life, others that the Centaur felt the suffering of Prometheus was worse than his own. Whatever the reason, the Centaur died, and his half-brother Jupiter placed him in Heaven where he has since been known as Sagittarius.

That was the end of Chiron myth proper, and yet the Centaur Chief still figures in our speech today, through words derived from ancient Greek. The Greek word *cheir*, which means hand, is a component not only of Chiron's name, but also of several words that serve to amplify the archetype of the Centaur Chief. It figures in chirog-

---

Prometheus, you will recall, was responsible for giving fire to humankind, an act which earned him Jupiter's wrath. In consequence, he was condemned eternal torture, unless one of the immortal gods would freely give up his own life to save that of Prometheus.

nomy, the ancient divinatory art popularly known as palmreading. It also figures in chirography, which means handwriting. Two forms of the healing art are derived from the root word *cheir*; namely chiropody (originally a term meaning the treatment of diseases of the hand and foot) and chiropractic (therapeutic treatment by means of manipulating the body, especially the spine). And finally there is chirurgery, a term which originally meant handiwork and then later came to mean surgery.

In all these etymological variations, key elements of the Chiron archetype are to be seen. For instance, chirognomy, as any palm reader will attest, is an oracular practice which depends in large part on astrology, through Planetary correspondences with parts of the hand. Chiron himself was known as an oracle and astrologer. Chirography echoes Chiron's function as a teacher, for it was through writing (originally handwriting) that cultural values have come to be passed down through the generations. Witness the distinction between history and prehistory. And chirurgery, chiropody and chiropractic are all forms of the healing art, for which Chiron was so well known. The latter in particular is perhaps most evocative today, because so many modern chiropractors believe in and practice the art of holistic medicine; that is, the technique of treating the whole individual rather than just his or her immediate symptoms.

At the bottom of all these derivations is *cheir*, the hand, which to my mind symbolizes Chiron's archetypal meaning as a holistic union of intellect and instinct, mind and body, human and animal. Perhaps the best illustration of this is to be found in something often said by artists; that in the creation of a work of art there is first the head and then no less important the hand. Something happens between the head and the hand, an artist once told me, that transforms and vitalizes the original conception. It's as if the hand has a mind of its own, an influence that in the final measure determines whether the work will be truly inspired or merely a technical exercise. Is this not the union of intellect and instinct, the very principle we see not only in Chiron's physical form as man-beast, but also in the way he taught his students? For he gave them not only technical skills, but ethical values as well. Under his tutelage, Jason and the others were not merely trained, they were prepared to act out their destinies in the best possible way.

Object Kowal took the formal name Chiron not by accident, but by virtue of a correspondence with the mythical archetype of the Centaur Chief. There are other elements of the Chiron archetype to be derived from the Minor Planet's astronomical and historical ana-

15

logs, as we shall see. From myth we learn that Chiron's astrological significance embraces the archetypes of Teacher, Healer, Musician, Hunter-Gatherer, Master Astrologer and Quest Guide. He symbolizes self-realization and fulfillment through a holistic union of reason and passion, intellect and instinct, animal and human. A blend of science and art is perfected in his nature. He is closely linked to his half brother Jupiter, the traditional ruler of Sagittarius and the ninth house — areas of the horoscope linked to quests of all kinds. And he is also associated with his father and grandfather, Saturn and Uranus respectively. It is too early at this point to formulate a full synthesis of Chiron's astrological archetype, but surely all the above-mentioned functions have a role to play.

CHAPTER 3

CHIRON TIME

How is the discovery of a new Planet incorporated into the astrological scheme of things? One answer is that it is not. Hindu astrologers, for example, constitute a clear majority of the world astrological community, and most of them to this day still practice the cosmic art/science without regard to any known Planets but the seven recognized since ancient times. These seven, the Sun, Moon, Mercury, Venus, Mars, Jupiter and Saturn, have been part of astrology since before the dawn of history.

Western astrology, on the other hand, has readily adapted to the discovery of new Planets. Virtually all American astrologers incorporate as part of their domain the three Planets discovered since the invention of the telescope. Quite a few also make use of the four principal Minor Planets, the asteroids, Ceres, Pallas, Juno and Vesta. And no small number of astrologers freely admit the importance of Planets that haven't even been discovered yet (and may never be discovered, for all we know), such as, for instance, hypothetical bodies like the Transneptunian Planets of the Uranian School of Astrology, the legendary intramercurial body Vulcan, the dark moon Lilith, and Transpluto (variously known as Bacchus/Dionysus or Persephone/Proserpine). In contrast to their Hindu counterparts, who are tradition-bound in the extreme, Western astrologers by and large are ready to accept the hypothesis that any Planetary body in our solar systems (no matter how recent its discovery) has astrological significance.

There will always be those who maintain that astrology is a traditional discipline, that all who would practice this discipline must restrict themselves only to the Planets that were known to Ptolemy

---

Astrologers use the term Planet — distinguished by an upper case P — to include the Sun and Moon, which are not planets in the astronomical sense of the word.

or some other archaic authority. But consider the Hermetic maxim, the cornerstone of astrology: "As Above, So Below". Of course, it means there is a correspondence between human affairs and the greater cosmos around us. But does this not imply that everything out there in the heavens has meaning in human terms?

Given the historic momentum of Western astrology, there can be no doubt that Chiron too will find a place of honor in the canons of horoscopy. Indeed, the process, has been underway for some time now. Already, ephemerides (tables of Planetary position) of Chiron are readily available to astrologers and their students. Popular computer astrology firms include Chiron in their commercial horoscopes, and interested parties have banded together to study the meaning of Chiron in astrological terms. (The Association for Studying Chiron was formed by a number of astrologers a year after Chiron's discovery, on November 13, 1978, at Warminster, Pennsylvania.)

How does one go about determining the astrological meaning of a newly discovered Planet? One very helpful clue is to be found in the historical milieu of the Planet's birth into human consciousness. To paraphrase Jung's Principle of Synchronicity, whatever is done or born at a given moment of time partakes of and reveals the essential meaning of that moment. The principle is far older than Jung, if you'll pardon the pun. Astrology *is* synchronicity, or it is nothing at all. The horoscope reveals the individual because it reveals the birth moment. The individual, the horoscope and the birth are three facets of the same reality.

When Uranus was discovered in 1781 (on March 13, to be specific), astrologers quite naturally looked to the historical context of the time as an expression of Uranus' meaning in human terms. What did they see? Revolution and emancipation, mostly. It was the year the tide of the American Revolution turned against the British. The Revolution of course predated Uranus' discovery and continued for some time therafter, but 1781 is generally considered the turning point in the struggle, the beginning of the end for English colonial interests in North America. America's ally in that revolution, the French, were not long in facing a revolution of their own. There was a quiet revolution going on in 1781 as well. It was the year Austria's serfs, by an edict of Joseph II, were emancipated. And throughout the Western world, the late 1700's were characterized by the Industrial Revolution, an ongoing process that has irrevocably altered the nature of human civilization. In view of these and similar historical signatures, astrologers quite naturally came to regard Uranus as symbolic of revolutionary changes, technological innovation and social equality.

The discovery of Neptune in 1846 was interpreted in much the same fashion. It was a time marked by idealism, exemplified in the transcendental school of literature in America. Into the social and political arena of that era came the *Communist Manifesto* of Marx and Engels, an idealistic philosophy that has since come to be regarded (most especially by those who have had to live under its influence) as a delusion. There was also a great interest in spiritualism at the time of Neptune's discovery. There were mediums and seances everywhere, and in the American West, the Mormons were busy with their very own exodus. In view of all these trends, astrologers came to regard Neptune as signifying idealism, psychism, spirituality — and a touch of delusion.

Following Pluto's discovery in 1930, astrologers looked around them and saw gangsterism on an unprecedented scale, from bank robbers to dictators. There was tremendous economic upheaval everywhere, and political power was concentrated into the hands of a few as never before in modern times. Soviet Russia labored under what was to be the first of many Five-Year Plans, at an appalling cost in human suffering. In Germany, the stage was set for Hitler, who was at that very moment refining his mad scheme for drawing the whole world into yet another apocalyptic bloodbath. Is it any wonder that astrologers came to regard Pluto as symbolic of force, power and regeneration through suffering?

If we apply the same approach to Chiron's discovery, what do we see? Initially, we might look at the actual date of Chiron's discovery, November 1, 1977, and then search the calendar of world history to find trends and events that could hold some clues as to the significance of the Centaur Planet. On that very date, for example, we note that U.S. President Jimmy Carter announced America's withdrawal from the International Labor Organization (I.L.O.). Two days later, French President Valery Giscard d'Estaing expressed support for French-speaking Quebec's right to self-determination — an action not favorably received by Canadian Prime Minister Pierre Ellioit Trudeau, to no one's surprise. And the following day, on November 4, the U.N. Security Council unanimously voted approval of a mandatory arms embargo against the Union of South Africa. Perhaps the biggest world news in the month of Chiron's discovery was made by Egyptian President Anwar Sadat and Israeli Prime Minister Menachem Begin, when they met and conferred in Jerusalem to discuss peace between their two nations on November 19, 1977. It was the beginning of a peace initiative that would eventually result in Egypt's isolation from her Arab neighbors, and it contributed in no small measure to Sadat's eventual assassination.

In more general terms, 1977 marked an era when, in the United States at least, there was a great deal of public attention focused on what has come to be called holistic medicine. Many doctors rejected the nation's conventional health care delivery system, and advocated a more all-encompassing approach to treating illness. Chiropractors and naturopathic physicians had been saying for years that it makes no sense to merely treat a specific symptom. The real solution, they insisted, was to treat the whole way of life that had brought that patient to a state of crisis in the first place. Restore the patient's life style to a condition of balance, they advised, and the symptoms would disappear — diet, exercise and peace of mind, they held, are crucial to physical health. It was an argument that caught on with many Americans in the late 1970's.

The middle and late 1970's, if we expand our perspective somewhat, offer a number of insights into Chiron's significance. In a tragic parallel to the mythical image of Chiron as the sufferer who could not die, there was the case of Karen Ann Quinlan. Miss Quinlan, who was in a coma as a result of a drug overdose, was the subject of a court battle that received nationwide attention. Her doctors advised that Miss Quinlan's case was hopeless, that if she were disconnected from her respirator she would die. The court agreed, and ruled that the respirator should be disconnected so as to allow Miss Quinlan the right to die with dignity. In 1976 the respirator was disconnected as ordered, but Karen did not die.

The late 1970's was also a time when public attention was focused on astrology by the unprecedented attack on the cosmic art/science initiated by 186 eminent scientists. Led by astronomer Dr. Bart Bok, the scientists deplored the public's fascination with astrology, and argued that the Hermetic Discipline did more harm than good. Their 1975 manifesto, "Objections to Astrology," only served to stimulate interest in the very subject they so vehemently deplored. Astrology made news in a more positive light in 1977, the year of Chiron's discovery, with the publication of *Recent Advances in Natal Astrology*, by Dr. Geoffrey Dean, and a world-wide team of collaborators. *Recent Advances* was widely hailed as the most important encyclopedic work on astrology since Ptolemy's *Tetrabiblos* was published in the 2nd Century. Although critical of many common astrological practices (and for that reason scathingly denounced by many practicing astrologers), *Recent Advances* clearly showed that there is solid scientific evidence to uphold the Hermetic hypothesis in general.

Looking back on the year of Chiron's discovery and the historical milieu of the late 1970's, it seems clear there are a number of themes that parallel the Chiron myth. There was a distinct focus on health and healing, for instance, echoing the image of Chiron the Healer. Chiron, the Master Astrologer, is represented as well, both negatively in terms of the attack by the 186 scientists, and quite positively in terms of Dr. Dean's *Recent Advances*. And in such political events as Egypt's isolation from her Arab allies, the rise of separatist sympathies in Quebec, the U.S. withdrawal from the I.L.O. and South Africa's quarantine from the world-at-large, one can see analogies to Chiron's position as the maverick of his race, the one and only Centaur who shunned the company of others of his kind to pursue what he felt was a better way of life.

Aside from symbolic events and trends at work in and around the year of Chiron's discovery, there are other key historical moments that serve to reveal the archetypal meaning of the Centaur Planet. One set of these moments has to do with Chiron's orbital cycle of perihelion and aphelion. The former moment coincides with Chiron's penetration of Saturn's orbit, the latter with Chiron's approach to the orbit of Uranus. One particularly interesting perihelion point of Chiron dates back to March 16, 1895. Ironically this is very close to the date when Chiron was first photographed (quite unconsciously at the time) on April 24, 1895. The 1895 perihelion point just happened to fall at six degrees and forty-five minutes of the sign Libra, less than five minutes of arc from an exact opposition to the natal Sun of a man who was to revolutionize the practice of modern medicine. The man's name is Wilhelm Roentgen, and he is remembered as the discoverer of X-rays. He was born on March 27, 1845, when Chiron was near its previous perihelion. In his natal horoscope you can see that Chiron occupies the Ascendant. (see Figure 1). One Chiron cycle after his birth, Roentgen discovered what he called "an invisible form of light," in 1895. In the years since, X-rays have become a standard part of medical practice.

Another notable contribution to the healing art was made by a man whose career parallels that of Roentgen in some respects. His name was Daniel Palmer, and he too was born in 1845, on March 7 to be specific (Unfortunately the time of Palmer's birth is not known to me, therefore I cannot furnish a natal horoscope.). Palmer drifted from one career to another for most of his life, passing time as a bee-keeper, a fishmonger and a grocer. Late in his variegated career he became a mesmerist, one who follows the teachings of Franz Anton Mesmer. In this capacity, Palmer treated illness through hypnosis, then known by the name Mesmer gave it, animal magnetism. On September 18, 1895 (the year of Chiron's perihelion, mind you), one Harvey Lillard came to Palmer's office seeking relief from a state of

21

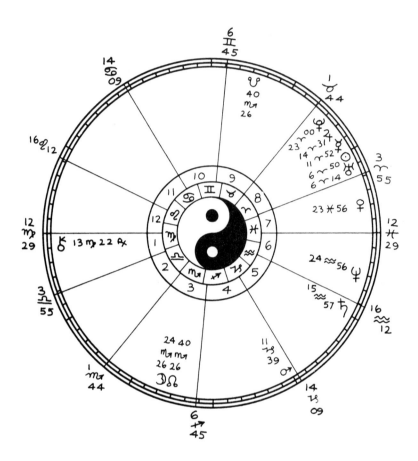

Figure 1. Natal horoscope (Tropical/Placidus) of Wilhem Roentgen, born 16:00 LMT (15:31:16 UT), March 27, 1845, at Lennep, Prussia (51N11, 7E11). Data source: *The Key*, No. 8 (March 10, 1980) and No. 14 (October 27, 1980).

total deafness which had afflicted him for the better part of twenty years. When the conventional animal magnetism treatments failed to work, Palmer discovered a misaligned vertebra in Lillard's spine. Manipulating the vertebra by hand with a sharp thrust, Palmer restored Lillard's hearing. Palmer's technique has since come to be known as chiropractic — an obvious link to Chiron the healer. Palmer's surname, it should be noted, is self-evidently linked to the Centaur. In another parallel to Chiron, who as we have noted previously was something of a loner, Palmer refused to apply for a medical license because he did not want to be associated with conventional doctors. To this day, chiropractic physicians remain virtual pariahs with respect to mainstream medicine.

Chiron's next perihelion took place on August 29, 1945, closely coinciding with the end of World War II. Germany's surrender to the Allies in Europe preceded the actual perihelion by several months, beginning on May 4 and culminating on May 8 (V-E Day). The Japanese surrender actually took place two weeks before the perihelion, on August 14; the formal surrender took place on the U.S.S. Missouri on September 2, 1945 (V-J Day). Japan's surrender was largely due to U.S. nuclear attacks on Hiroshima (August 6) and Nagasaki (August 9). Both of these attacks were made possible by the first atomic bomb test, which occurred on July 16, 1945. Recalling the legend of Chiron as a master of the arts of war, yet always one who preferred peace, it seems only fitting that the end of World War II should coincide with a significant moment in Chiron's orbital cycle. After all, that war did result in the defeat of all the aggressors save one — lest we forget, the invasion of Poland which began the war was a two-pronged attack by Germany and the Soviet Union. Considered in relation to the end of World War II, Chiron's perihelion recalls the myth of Prometheus, the god for whom the Centaur gave up his immortality. In this case, the scientists who developed the atomic bomb (individually and collectively) play the role of Prometheus, giving to humanity an advanced form of technology dealing with powers so great that their misuse could be disastrous.

How has Promethean science redeemed its atomic fire, if at all? The Chiron myth says that redemption comes through healing, for it was the Centaur who redeemed Prometheus. It also tells us that the Healer must be sacrificed in the act of healing — the personal commitment to self-sacrifice is always in its own terms total, although it does not in every case necessarily culminate in an obvious moment of self-destruction. The ultimate result is, in any case, always a mixture of the tragic and the sublime — the Centaur gives up his biological life, but retains his immortality in the heavens. Perhaps there

23

was a hopeful, healing momentum signified by the 1945 Chiron perihelion, even though it also coincided with the climax of a global bloodbath. It was in 1945, for example, that Dr. Jonas Salk was working on his virus-typing research at the University of Pittsburgh. Dr. Salk's studies, generously funded by the National Foundation Virus Research Committee, led to the development of a vaccine which has virtually eliminated poliomyelitis. Might this not be an indication of the way Chiron the Healer can redeem Prometheus the Scientist? By the time of the next Chiron perihelion, on February 14, 1996 (St. Valentine's Day, a hopeful omen?), it should be clear whether redemption can be accomplished in this century.

Chiron's aphelion seems to have a character quite distinct from the perihelion. I believe the principal difference is symbolized by the two orbits with which Chiron is so closely linked. At perihelion, Chiron penetrates Saturn's orbit, crystallizing the Centaur's archetype in a way that favors technical handiwork. Whether these technological wonders are medical or military (or musical, or astrological, or educational, for these are all Chiron archetypes) makes no difference. The point is that Saturn is earthy in nature, therefore Chiron's penetration of Saturn's orbit favors concrete and material development. At aphelion, on the other hand, Chiron approaches the orbit of Uranus. Whereas Saturn is conservative and developmental in nature, Uranus is just the opposite — revolutionary and innovative, social and intellectual rather than materialistic. Consequently Chiron's aphelion signifies a time of great emphasis on social change, rather than technical consolidation — of breakthrough, rather than culmination.

Looking back on the June 2, 1920, Chiron aphelion, for instance, we see the adoption of the 19th Amendment to the U.S. Constitution, giving women the right to vote nationwide for the first time in American history. The 19th Amendment had been adopted by Congress in 1918-1919. It was ratified by Tennessee on August 18, 1920, and proclaimed officially in effect by U.S. Secretary of State Bainbridge Colby on August 26, 1920. This was a landmark in the struggle for women's rights, and a harbinger of great things to come. Although the pace of social change was terribly slow at first, the 19th Amendment gave impetus to the recognition of women as full citizens and complete human beings. Of course the struggle continues today, and there remains a great deal to be accomplished before true equality between the sexes is a reality. But the adoption of the 19th Amendment coincident with Chiron's aphelion appears in retrospect to be a highly significant development in this ongoing crusade. It brings to mind Chiron's mythical nature as a union of opposites, a wise being who affirmed both polarities of existence, just as the women's rights movement has sought to insure equality between the two sexes. The 1920 aphelion also coincided with the first meeting of the League of Nations at Geneva, Switzerland. Formed in the hope that it might help to prevent the reoccurrence of a world war such as the one that had just ended, the League of Nations was a most idealistic venture. However it never achieved the status its founders had hoped for, and was a self-evident failure when it came to preventing World War II. Ironically, the League of Nations' successor, the United Nations, was formally organized at Chiron's perihelion in 1945. The revolutionary impetus that surfaced at the 1920 aphelion thus took on more substantial form at the 1945 perihelion.

The December 7, 1970 Chiron aphelion also seems to have signified an advance in the struggle for human rights in general and women's rights in particular. It was in that year that President Nixon named the first women generals in U.S. history, with the promotion of Col. Elizabeth Hoisington and Col. Anna Hays to the rank of brigadier general in the army. Work on behalf of the women's movement continued apace that year, reaching a watershed point fifteen months later with Senate approval of the Equal Rights Amendment. Another significant moment in the year of Chiron's aphelion was the first Earth Day, celebrated on April 22, 1970 (the first Full Moon after Sol's entry into the earth sign Taurus that year). It focused attention on the pressing need to protect the earth from ecological damage, especially pollution — paralleling Chiron's mythical suffering from another kind of poison. And just three months after the aphelion came Senate approval of the 26th Amendment, lowering the voting age in all elections to eighteen.

The examples cited heretofore are necessarily only a brief sampling of historical events connected with key moments relating to Chiron's discovery and orbital cycles. While these examples may serve to illustrate how Chiron's meaning might be interpreted through reference to history, they are in reality only a derivative means of astrological interpretation. For a more direct interpretation, we have only to consult the chart that represents Chiron's birth into human consciousness as a Planet — Chiron's natal horoscope, as it were (see Figure 2). As with any horoscope, there is virtually no limit to the amount of information represented by this chart. Rather than attempt an exhaustive interpretation of the birth chart, let us examine only a few key elements, to see what they suggest about Chiron's astrological significance.

25

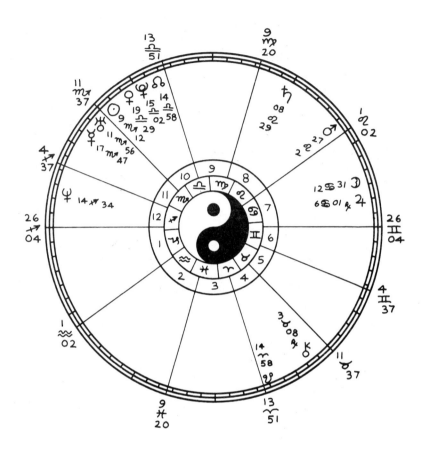

Figure 2. Horoscope (Tropical/Placidus) of Chiron's discovery, 10:00 PST (18:00 UT), November 1, 1977, at Pasadena, California (34N09, 118W09). Data source: *The Key*, No. 16 (January 10, 1981).

Of immediate interest is Chiron's position in the chart, at three degrees and eight minutes of the sign Taurus. An often helpful means of interpreting individual degree significance is afforded by the so-called Sabian symbols, originally developed by astrologer Marc Edmund Jones and psychic medium Elsie Wheeler in 1925. This oracle assigns a characteristic symbol for each degree of the zodiac. Degrees are always rounded up for the purposes of Sabian analysis — thus any position between three degrees Taurus and three degrees Taurus fifty-nine minutes and fifty-nine seconds would be considered the fourth degree of Taurus. With this in mind, the Sabian symbol for Chiron's discovery position is the proverbial 'pot of gold at the rainbow's end,' suggesting that Chiron holds great promise of some kind. In his book, *An Astrological Mandala*, Dane Rudhyar keynotes this degree as meaning the plenitude that flows from connecting the celestial and heavenly natures, and further suggests that it points to some sort of transubstantiation of matter.

I believe this is a most appropriate representation of Chiron's meaning in human terms. The Centaur is after all a union of opposites, much like a bridge between heaven and earth. As the Quest Guide, Chiron does promise both transmutation of matter (creating from ordinary mortals real mythic heroes) and the pot of gold at the end of the rainbow (the achievement of the Quest). In this regard the Sabian symbol for the Ascendant in Chiron's discovery chart seems especially significant. The 27th degree of Sagittarius rises in this chart, symbolizing the personal identity Chiron projects into this world. In Sabian parlance, this degree is represented by a sculptor at work, a clear indication of the ability we humans have to transform raw matter in accordance with our own personal vision. Is this not what the great heroes of Greek myth did, under Chiron's tutelage? These are clear and unmistakable symbolic images, suggesting in no uncertain terms that Chiron means for each of us a real and practical potential for self-transformation of the most radical kind — the kind that leads us to a full awareness of and capacity for our personal identity and mission in this life.

One could go on indefinitely analyzing the Sabian symbols for specific degrees in Chiron's discovery chart. In addition to the Sun and Ascendant, the Moon's degree could also be considered — these three, after all, are generally regarded as fundamental indicators in any horoscope. In this connection it is symbolically appropriate that the Sabian symbol for the Moon in the discovery chart (at 13 degrees Cancer) is "a hand with a prominent thumb is held out for study." I find this curiously appropriate because the name Chiron

27

itself is derived, you will recall, from the Greek word *cheir*, which means hand. However at this point I see no need to indulge in Sabian overkill. It is enough that we have been pointed in the right direction, towards an understanding of Chiron as having to do with, on the one hand a bridge between the mundane and the spiritual, and on the other hand as symbolic of the alchemical "Great Work" of self-transformation.

CHAPTER 4

THE ASTROLOGER'S ASTROLOGER

To understand Chiron's astrological significance it is necessary, at the very least, to synthesize the astronomical, mythical and historical functions that characterize the Centaur Planet. These three qualities are as many different ways of approaching the same phenomenon. Any one of them considered in isolation from the others is potentially misleading, but taken together they point the way to a fundamental archetype in the absence of which astrology itself is incomplete. Chiron is a complex astrological function, a whole embracing many parts any one of which may seem unrelated to the others. Nevertheless, there is an identity behind all the seeming multiplicity. As we consider key elements of the Chiron archetype one at a time, Dear Reader, be on the lookout for the unifying principle that underlies all the disparate parts.

Chiron is a Planet having to do with mental processes. Mythology tells us that the Chief Centaur was renowned for his wisdom. History associates Chiron with intellectual breakthroughs (such as Roentgen's discovery of X-rays) and idealism (the founding of the League of Nations and the United Nations, as well as the women's rights movement). Astronomy tells us on the one hand that Chiron has no atmosphere, and on the other that an atmosphere distorts and obscures perception (a mental process) of the celestial world.

Astronomy also tells us that Chiron has an extreme inclination to the ecliptic plane, a factor the Centaur Planet shares with Mercury and Pluto. Mercury is universally regarded among astrologers as a Planet of the mind, and Pluto is said to connote (among other things) investigation of what is hidden, which implies a mental process. In all three cases, extremes of ecliptic inclination result in the Planet rising far north and sinking far south of the ecliptic plane, hence suggesting a great deal of perspective. This perspective is common to all three Planets, and I believe it symbolizes an essential quality of consciousness inherent in all mental processes; namely the ability to adopt an unusual vantage point, to rise above oneself, as it were. In this regard it is interesting to note that of the four major asteroids commonly used by astrologers, the one with the greatest inclination to the ecliptic is also the only one Mythology associates with mental processes — namely Pallas. Pallas Athena was considered the goddess of reason and wisdom

Although symbolic of mentality, Chiron has nothing to do with pie-in-the-sky ivory tower intellectualism. Some thought processes are ends in themselves, others are means to an end — Chiron signifies the latter category. In myth the Centaur trained his pupils for an objective, which was always to pursue a Quest of destiny. And he was not satisfied merely to give his wards the special instruction they would need to overcome particular obstacles. Rather he sought to give them all kinds of training, including an ethical education, in order that they would be generalists instead of specialists, holistic rather than reductionist. This condition of practical wholeness was regarded by Chiron as an essential quality of the fully realized human being (hero). It characterizes the kind of mentality signified by Chiron, a balanced blend of idealism and practicality.

In the same fashion, Chiron's historical association with women's rights and supranational government speaks of an idealism that is at once holistic and practical. Peace and equality are dreams of long standing, but without such developments as these they would be nothing more than beautiful ideals. They are still dreams, of course, being far from fully realized in actual fact. And yet it is now no longer a mere dream that women can vote; and while there is still war, there are also U.N. peacekeeping troops deployed in various global trouble spots to hold opposing sides apart.

In astronomical terms, Chiron's transorbital shuttling from Saturn to Uranus also takes on an aspect of holism, of practical idealism. Saturn is conservative, materialistic and practical, while Uranus is revolutionary, social and idealistic. To unite these two opposites, as Chiron does through its orbit, is to create a holistic form of consciousness that transcends the tension between them. If Saturn be the thesis and Uranus the antithesis, then Chiron is the synthesis that affirms both polarities while at the same time reconciling their conflict. Thus Chiron symbolizes a kind of link or bridge — or a rainbow between heaven and earth, to use a Sabian metaphor.

Mythology also tells us that Chiron was a loner. Although the first of his hybrid species and the acknowledged chief of all the Centaurs, Chiron preferred to be a hermit at Mt. Pelion, where he devoted himself to the pursuit of his mission in life. In astronomy the

Centaur Planet is also a loner. There may very well be other Minor Planets plying orbits similar to Chiron's but only one such Planet has been discovered to date. If mythology is any indication, there can be no doubt that other Minor Planets similar to Chiron will be discovered in time. Those to follow will be Centaurs too, but there can only be one Chiron. In its historical correlation to David Palmer, the father of modern chiropractic healing, Chiron's maverick quality is further emphasized. Palmer, after all, refused to be associated with other doctors. These correspondences all point to Chiron as symbolic of separatism, isolationism and withdrawal of various kinds.

Chiron's mythical role as teacher, mentor and guardian in relation to the legendary heroes of ancient Greece is full of symbolic import. It is echoed in the astronomical relationship of Chiron to Saturn and Uranus, for the best teacher is one who imparts an understanding of what is and has been (Saturn), while at the same time preparing the student to accept a role in creating what is to come (Uranus). History adds its testimony on behalf of Chiron's link to teaching, telling us that David Palmer was the founder of the modern school of chiropractic healing. The best teacher is always more than a mere instructor transmitting information. The best teacher goes beyond simply preparing his students — he inspires them as well, thus becoming a true mentor. Astrologers generally associate teaching with Mercury, the Planet that is said to rule the transmission of mental impulses. This may be true with regard to ordinary teachers, but when it comes to the really great teacher, Mercury is left far behind. Until the discovery of Chiron, astrology had no interpretive function to signify a true mentor, a truly great teacher — that day is now behind us.

I have said that although Chiron signifies mental processes, these are not to be associated with impractical idealism. This is not meant to disparage pure thought as opposed to applied thought — both have their value of course. Rather I mean to emphasize that Chiron is associated with concrete and practical thought which aims to effect a real impact on the material world, to transform the environment in some way or another. The myth of Chiron the Healer affords an excellent illustration of the difference between these two kinds of mental activity. Certainly any healer must have some knowledge of anatomy — but so must a classical painter. The healer uses this knowledge to save lives, the artist to enrich them. Both are worthy objectives, but only one of them is normally a life-and-death struggle for anyone other than the practitioner himself or herself. It is true that Chiron, ever the holistic Centaur, was an artist, for he was renowned as a master of the lyre. But he was also a healer, and that we must not forget.

Chiron's historical link to health and healing is obvious in light of X-rays and chiropractic therapy. Chiron's penetration of Saturn's orbit is noteworthy in this regard. Saturn, astrology tells us, is the Planet that times the ticking of our life-clocks. Every Planet plays a role in the unfolding of our lives to be sure, but Saturn alone is mythically linked to the aging process. In myth, the old god Saturn is regarded as Father Time. Modern science tells us that aging eventually saps the body's ability to renew itself, a process that ultimately results in death. Of all the Planets known today, there is only one which acts as a link between physical degeneration (Saturn) and revolutionary discoveries (Uranus). That Planet is, of course, Chiron, the sole astrological function that is mythically assigned the task of reversing degenerative processes regardless of whether these are due to injury or illness.

The power to heal is also the power to kill, and so we should remember that Chiron was no less a master of the martial arts than he was a physician. The greatest heroes of Greek myth learned to hunt, ride and fight at the Centaur's cave. From the carnage at Troy to the slaughter at the field of Ares in Colchis, Chiron's pupils distinguished themselves in the ghastly art of killing. Those of us who think of ourselves as peace-loving cannot help but be appalled at this aspect of the Centaur. How could a being so wise, so just and humane, be capable of inspiring atrocities such as these? I can only answer that Chiron is the very essence of holism, and that like everything else holism is a triune phenomenon — creation, preservation and destruction are its triple manifestations. Violence is a fact of life in the material world, and therefore the Centaur mastered it as he did so many things. And yet the heroes to whom he taught the martial virtues were not wanton killers. They fought to protect the innocent, to avenge the powerless. They fought with honor, and they were ready to die without regrets. A modern analogy might be the civilized response to terrorism, which is to save the victims even if it means killing some of the perpetrators.

The historical correlation of Chiron's perihelion with the nuclear attacks on Japan at the end of World War II may be seen as an example of the Centaur's martial aspect. Those two bombs were weapons of horrible destruction, created through applied intelligence. They were monstrously effective, and killed as many as a quarter million human beings according to some estimates. (Other estimates place the death toll as low as half that.) And yet without those two bombs the war could have dragged on much longer, resulting in even more casualties. It is a sad commentary on the state of human affairs that a nuclear attack could ever be the more humane of two options, and yet that is precisely the ghastly dilemma President Harry Truman had to face. Truman has since been condemned for the choice he made, by people who have the luxury of hindsight and the incalculable advantage of never having to make such an awful decision themselves. It was a forced choice between two evils, and somehow the fact that it coincided with Chiron's perihelion inclines me to believe that President Truman opted for the lesser horror.

Chiron's multifaceted archetype also touches on astrology. Mythology tells us that the Centaur Chief taught astrology to the hero Hercules and the heroic physician Asclepius. History relates Chiron to important developments in astrology around the time of this Minor Planet's discovery. Astrologers traditionally associate their discipline with the Planet Uranus, and astronomy tells us that Chiron's orbit is closely related to that Planet. Surely Uranus, as the archetypal god of the celestial sphere, deserves recognition as central to astrology. But by the same token, Chiron ought to be seen as the Planet, if not of astrology, then of astrologers. Myth never speaks of Uranus practicing or teaching the cosmic art/science, whereas Chiron is recognized in legend as the astrologer's astrologer.

Astrology is the original holistic discipline, teaching as it does the indivisible union of heaven and earth. The Hermetic Maxim postulates that we and the celestial environment are one whole organism, a sentient being. The sage, if I may be allowed to mix metaphors taken from Taoism and astrology, is one who recognizes the unity of humankind and the cosmos, and who learns to consciously pattern the personal life in harmony with the celestial. This may be done in one of two basic ways. One might take a passive approach to astrology, looking to the heavens for descriptions of what one is (character) and what events are likely to be encountered in one's life (destiny). This is not the sort of astrology Chiron signifies. The higher road, the path symbolized by the Sabian symbol of Chiron's discovery degree (a rainbow linking heaven and earth) is not at all passive. Instead, this sort of astrology looks to the heavens as symbolic not only of what one is, but what one might become; not only of what might happen to oneself, but what one might bring to light in a creative way.

Astrology as it is commonly practiced is descriptive and fatalistic. It is used as a means to uncover a supposedly immutable character, to reveal a destiny which is more or less likely to happen. The astrology symbolized by Chiron is on the other hand creative and transformative. It doesn't tell you merely what you are in terms of so many character traits. It doesn't lay out for you a map of so many alternative realities, some combination of which will prove to be your fate. Chiron, let us remember, was a mentor, someone to whom people came in preparation for heroic deeds. The ultimate act of heroism is the transformation of self, the creation of destiny through the transcendence of fate. It is this creative, alchemical sort of astrology that Chiron signifies.

Remember the legend of Jason, how he came to Chiron as a result of events that were set into motion before he was born? The Centaur saw Jason's karma, his fated inertia, but he also saw the child's dharma, the path of action whereby the son of Aeson could redeem himself and thereby overcome his fate. Who would have thought that a child abandoned and ostracized would someday undertake a heroic quest that would end up rectifying karmic imbalances from out of the past? The Centaur knew it could come to pass, he prepared the child in every sense of the word, and ultimately it really happened. In much the same fashion, the kind of astrology Chiron represents is transformative. It is a kind of cosmic alchemy, transmuting the leaden fate of the individual into the pot of gold at the end of the rainbow.

Let me give you an example of the way Chiron works. When the time had come for Jason to begin his Quest, the Centaur said not a word. He could tell Jason was restless, and he knew why, but he did nothing to prompt his pupil. They stood together on the peak of Mt. Pelion, looking out over Jason's homeland. The young man told the Centaur that he longed to go back and win the kingdom that was rightfully his. Chiron advised him of the dangers inherent in such a venture, but the youth would not be dissuaded. "If you must go," the Centaur said, "promise me two things: speak harshly to no one whom you shall meet, and stand by the words you speak." Jason promised, and then he was gone.

Coming down from Mt. Pelion, Jason found himself at the banks of the river Anauros, which was then swollen with swift floodwaters. An old and feeble woman sat there at the river's edge, and asked Jason to carry her across the torrent. Being young and brash, Jason was inclined to scorn the old woman's request, but then he remembered the first of the two promises he had made to Chiron. So he took her on his back and plunged into the river. The footing was treacherous, the current wild and overpowering, and Jason immediately had second thoughts about his good deed. It would be next to impossible to wade through the river alone, much less carrying someone else. He was inclined to renege on his commitment to the old woman, but he remembered his second promise to the Centaur

34

and kept going. At last he managed to stagger onto the opposite shore. He set the old woman down, and fell gasping and exhausted on the riverbank. Then a miracle happened. The old woman was transformed into Juno herself, wife of Jupiter and Queen of Heaven. She announced herself to the awestruck Jason, and pledged to repay his kindness. Much later, when Jason and the Argonauts were engaged in the perilous Quest for the Golden Fleece, Juno's help proved to be indispensable.

More than a quaint old story, this myth is an illustration of the way Chiron transforms the oracular potential of astrology. Chiron was known as a prophet, and as an astrologer. Yet he did not directly foretell in so many words what would happen to Jason, nor did he say that Jason was inclined to be brash or intolerant of those who were not as young and as strong as he. A lesser astrologer might have proceeded to foretell Jason's future and delineate his character in just such terms as these, but not Chiron. Instead the Centaur impressed upon his ward the importance of ethical standards that ended up serving him far better than mere foreknowledge ever could. Chiron *transformed* Jason, and thus enabled his student to embark on the Quest that changed his life forever and for the better.

Call him a mentor, a teacher, a guru, Guide, Psychopomp, Initiator or whatever you like, Chiron played all these roles to the hilt, and then he went one step farther — he died. In giving up his immortality to save another, the Centaur revealed his ultimate secret. Mythology tells that all Chiron's students came to him as children, just as each of us must become as children again in order to be transformed. As anyone who has ever been a parent can testify, children place an almost supernatural faith in their teachers. But sooner or later there must come a time when the child will sacrifice the godlike image of the teacher in order to take on an identity of its own. In mythological terms, the teacher must die in order for the student to truly live; otherwise the student forges an unhealthy dependence on the teacher, and consequently gets frozen in an arrested stage of development. By making the ultimate sacrifice, the Centaur was telling us that the True Guide is to be found not outside of ourselves, but within.

We have seen a number of life functions that correspond to the Chiron archetype thus far — healer, astrologer, teacher, mentor, guide, a synthesis of dialectical opposites, a practical intellect, holism, a bridge, a link, etc. Perhaps the most comprehensive archetype of the Centaur is the one we have not yet considered. It is suggested by the graphic symbol for the Centaur Planet, which resembles the letter O surmounted by the letter K. (There is another Chiron glyph also in use, ♀, but the ⚷ symbol seems to have greater currency in the astrological community, if only by virtue of its adoption by the Association for Studying Chiron.) The origin of this simple glyph is obvious enough. The O stands for Object, the K for Kowal. However the symbolism is archetypally appropriate: ⚷ is a stylized key. Look at it phenomenologically, and the meaning becomes clear. A key is a device used to open a passageway from one reality to another. That, in essence, is just what Chiron represents.

Much has been written in recent years about the possibility of using astrology as a means for self-transformation. However all we have been told so far is that transformative astrology is something you think about until you learn how to do it. Have you ever succeeded in learning something just by thinking about it? Granted, it can be done — but isn't it easier to learn by doing? As an astrological archetype, Chiron holds forth the promise of self-transformation through a synthetic, holistic union of thought and action. The Centaur Planet is an alchemical key to be found within each of us. Potential uses for this key are limited only by the individual who finds it. To discover how Chiron's key fits into your life, Dear Reader, you have only to examine your natal horoscope.

CHAPTER 5

ON THE WAY TO PELION

The Centaur Planet, we have seen, stands for a synthesis of thought and action. To become acquainted with Chiron's meaning in the natal horoscope is therefore more than simply a mental process, more than merely an assimilation of information. A true grounding in Chiron's astrological significance must ultimately lead to a dialogue, an active meeting of minds. You can achieve mastery of most astrological functions just by learning about them, but with Chiron the learning is only the beginning, only an orientation. It is much like the problem Jason faced in coming to know the Centaur Chief. First he had to find his way up Mt. Pelion, and only then was he in a position to meet his mentor.

While Chiron is ultimately a holistic astrological function, the path whereby one comes to know the Centaur Chief requires a limited perspective. This is because the reality Chiron represents is so all-encompassing that it can be perceived only a little bit at a time, at least in the initial stages. How could you learn to bake a cake, for example, unless you first learn what flour is, what a measuring cup is, what sugar is, etc.? Or how could you learn to change a flat tire on your car, without first knowing what a lug nut is, what a jack is, where the spare is kept, etc.? These mundane examples illustrate what ought to be a perfectly self-evident point; namely that learning any whole function requires mastery of the component parts thereof. This may seem to be the very antithesis of holism, but it is necessary nonetheless.

Coming to know Chiron a little at a time requires constant reference to the whole function represented by the Centaur Planet. To repeat all the various elements of that function every step of the way would not only be terribly laborious and time-consuming, but it would also prevent you, Dear Reader, from assimilating the totality of Chiron's meaning. Therefore it will be helpful to think of just a few archetypal functions as representative of Chiron. Such concepts as the mentor, self-transformation and the Quest come as close as anything to expressing the quintessence of the Centaur Chief. For the time being let us use these admittedly limited concepts as tokens of the whole that is Chiron. Should you feel the need to replenish your feel for Chiron's more comprehensive symbolism at any step along the way, feel free to refer to Chapters 1 through 4.

The best way to get oriented to the Centaur Planet is to start with its most obvious relationships with respect to the birth chart as a whole. Most basic of these is Chiron's relationship to the horizon, whether above or below it. Experienced students of astrology can of course determine this fundamental factor at a glance, and in fact it is very easy to do. The horizon is the line between the Ascendant (cusp of the first house) and the Descendant (cusp of the seventh house). It divides the chart into two halves, upper and lower. The half above is the diurnal half, that portion of the heavens which was above the horizon at your birth. The half below is the nocturnal hemisphere, that segment of the celestial sphere which was below the horizon when you were born. If located in houses one through six in your birth chart, Chiron was nocturnal at your birth. If posited in houses seven through twelve in your natal horoscope, Chiron was diurnal at your nativity.

Nocturnal Chiron is in the realm of the subjective, the psychic, the reality that is felt rather than seen. Such an individual is more likely to play the role of a mentor than someone born under the aegis of the diurnal Chiron. Granted, we are all students, we all have a mentor at one time or another, and sooner or later we are certain to serve as someone else's mentor. Even if we are not expressly aware of these things, they are objectively true. Nocturnal Chiron natives tend to be psychically attuned to the mentor within, and less likely to search for a True Guide outside themselves. Often they are unconscious of the mentor function in their lives, and yet by what seems to be only happenstance they are drawn into circumstances that lead them to an awareness of their potential for self-transformation. Actually it is not simple chance that brings on this metamorphosis. Rather it is a subconscious yearning that works below the level of rational awareness to produce opportunities for transcendent growth. Or it may be only a half-conscious phenomenon, a vaguely felt restlessness that impels the individual toward an altered state of consciousness.

Examples of the nocturnal Chiron are many and instructive. A particularly interesting triad is comprised of Sigmund Freud, his protégé, Carl Jung, and Jung's erstwhile patient, Herman Hesse.

38

Freud is, of course, the acknowledged founder of modern psychoanalysis, whose exploration of the subconscious levels of human awareness revolutionized our understanding of personal dynamics. (See Freud's natal horoscope, Figure 3). Jung in a sense turned Freud's theory on its head. "It is we who subsist in the unconscious," Jung said, "and not the other way around" (see Jung's birth chart, Figure 4). Hermann Hesse became a cult figure guru through his many novels, the best known of which was *Siddhartha*, the story of one man's relationship to the mentor-function that lies within each of us (for Hesse's birth chart, see Figure 5). All three of these individuals became gurus to millions who sought to transform themselves by way of the path that leads within. Other examples of nocturnal Chiron include Werner Erhard, the founder of EST, existentialist Jean Paul Sartre, and a host of variegated gurus such as Yogananda Paramahansa, Karl Marx, Nicolai Lenin, nonviolent political leaders Mohandas (Mahatma) Gandhi and Martin Luther King, Jr., and Mormon patriarchs Joseph Smith and Brigham Young; also Beatle John Lennon (see Figure 6), who was hailed as a guru of sorts by millions of young people in the 1960's and 1970's.

A diurnal Chiron in the natal horoscope represents a diametrically opposite orientation to the possibilities signified by the Centaur Planet. This individual tends to project the Chiron function outward from the self onto others. Instead of independently initiating the process that leads toward a confrontation with the mentor within, this person is more likely to be the apparent beneficiary of contacts with other people who will serve in the role of a mentor. There is paradoxically a heightened awareness of the need for self-transformation, yet at the same time there is a feeling that someone or something else outside the self must act to catalyze this metamorphosis. This often leads to a sense of searching, a tendency to place inordinate faith in external gurus or institutions. Any personal metamorphosis is facilitated by a long journey of one kind or another, and this is especially important to those born under the diurnal Chiron. In the extreme case, this can manifest as a kind of compulsive wandering in search of some paradisical environment where the individual feels that circumstances will promote a miraculous self-transformation.

Examples of the diurnal Chiron include several cult heroes from the contemporary scene, all of whom exhibit in some measure a transformative wanderlust or a notable projection of the mentor function outward from the self onto other people or instituions. For instance, there is singer/songwriter Bob Dylan, whose wanderlust contributed to his near-fatal motorcycle accident in the 1960's, and who later sought an external mentor by way of his conversion to

Figure 3. Natal horoscope (Tropical/Placidus) of Sigmund Freud, born 18:30 LMT (17:17:24 UT), May 6, 1856, at Freiberg, Germany (49N38, 18E09). Data source: Lois M. Rodden, *American Book of Charts*. San Diego, CA: Astro Computing Services, 1980. (This source hereafter designated LMR, ABC.)

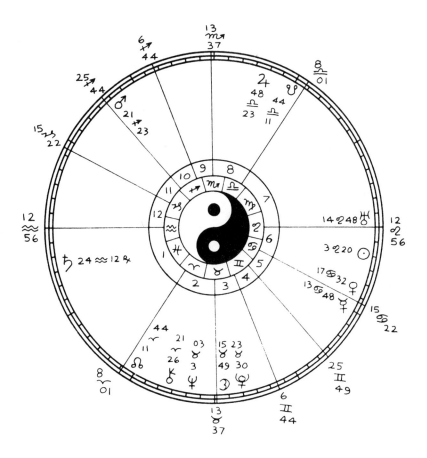

Figure 4. Natal horoscope (Tropical/Pacidus) of Carl Jung, born 19:26 GMT, July 26, 1875, at Kesswill Switzerland (47N36, 9E19) Data source: LMR, ABC.

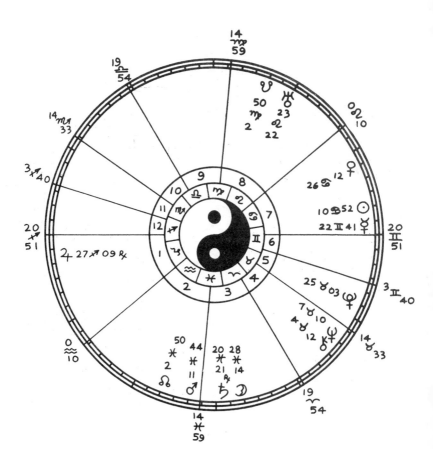

Figure 5. Natal horoscope (Tropical/Placidus) of Hermann Hesse,
born 18:30 LMT (17:57:48 UT), July 2, 1877, at Calw,
Wuertenburg, Germany (48N00, 8E03). Data source:
LMR, ABC.

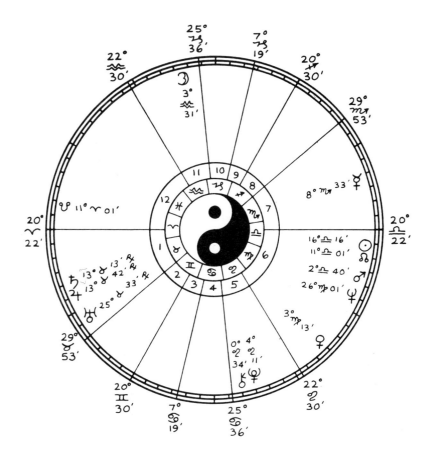

Figure 6. Natal horoscope (Tropical/Placidus) of John Lennon, born 6:30 p.m. British Summer Time (17:30 UT), October 9, 1940, at Liverpool, England (53N25, 02W58). Data source: Lois Rodden, January 1, 1982, Errata to *American Book of Charts*. Data classification: A.

Christian fundamentalism (see Dylan's natal horoscope, Figure 7). And then there is Carlos Castaneda, author of the popular Don Juan fantasies, who was born in Peru and then moved to the United States, where he wrote his fanciful accounts of a Mexican shaman (for Castaneda's birth chart, see Figure 8). Here we have both a long journey and a projection of the mentor archetype outward from the self onto a fictional Mexican brujo. Additional examples include "Beat" novelist Jack Kerouac, pop guru Ram Dass (née psychedelic advocate Dr. Richard Alpert), and theologian/musician/doctor Albert Schweitzer.

The Ascendant-Descendant axis establishes one fundamental set of hemispheres in the birth chart, but this is not the only important dichotomy. The axis from the tenth house cusp (the Midheaven or Medium Coeli, abbreviated MC) to the fourth house cusp (the Imum Coeli, abbreviated IC) also comprises a key division of the horoscope. Whereas the basic symbolism of the horizontally-divided hemispheres derives from the archetypal concepts of above and below, sky and earth, the symbolic nature of the meridianally-separated hemispheres follows from the fact that the meridian distinguishes left from right, rising from setting. Look at any birth chart, and you can see this for yourself. The part of the horoscope to the left of the meridian (houses 1-3 and 10-12) rises, while that part to the right (houses 4-9) is setting. Depending on which of these two hemispheres Chiron occupies in the birth chart, there can be two fundamentally different expressions of the Centaur Planet's archetype in the individual's life.

Chiron in the rising hemisphere signifies one who tends to emphasize the more intuitive and idealistic possibilities of the Centaur Planet's archetype, generally at the expense of the more practical element which is nonetheless always a part of this function. Such an individual excels more in the social and intellectual arena than in the materialistic and practical, all else being equal. Granted, with Chiron there always exists a bridge between these two opposing poles — this placement indicates only an emphasis on one polarity, not a total exclusion of the other. A person born with Chiron in the left hemisphere, for example, may be better at teaching healing than at practicing the healing art; or better at astrological research than astrological counseling.

The all important mentor function signified by the Centaur Planet takes on a special character for individuals who are born with Chiron in the rising hemisphere. They tend to expect their mentor to be recognizable at a glance, as it were, as if some outstanding charismatic quality of the mentor should be able to reach

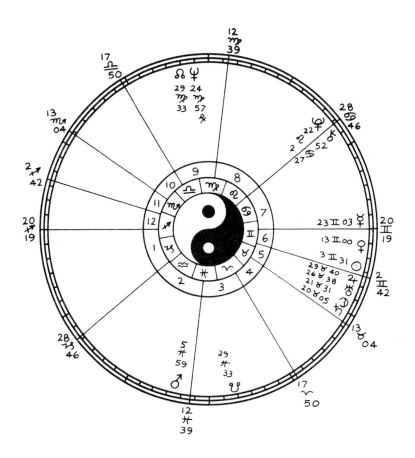

Figure 7. Natal horoscope (Tropical/Placidus) of Bob Dylan, born
21:05 CST (03:05 UT May 25), May 24, 1941, at Duluth,
Minnesota (46N47, 92W07). Data source. LMR, ABC.

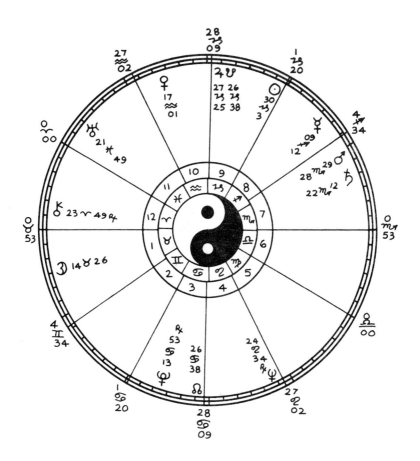

Figure 8. Natal horoscope (Tropical/Placidus) of Carlos Castaneda, born 14:00 EST (19:00 UT), December 25, 1925, at Cajamarca, Peru (7S10, 78W31). Data source: LMR, ABC.

out and bowl them over in an instant, on first sight. It is often important for these people to learn to distinguish between flashy charisma and real character, and in this regard the most important criterion is ethical: Chiron is always charismatic (not always flashy!) and always ethical. Thus, for instance, if you were born under this Chiron hemisphere emphasis and find yourself drawn to a mentor (whether subjective or objective in appearance) who combines charismatic appeal with questionable ethical standards, you would be well advised to beat a hasty retreat despite any and all other inclinations to the contrary.

Examples of left-hemisphere Chiron natives include a number of individuals who are remembered in large part because of their involvement with unusual (not to mention controversial) causes. For instance there is Uri Geller, the Israeli psychic superstar who caused such a stir in the 1970's with his spoonbending feats. Supporters (and they included some scientists) believed Uri's claim that his mind-over-matter demonstrations were just that. Critics charged that Geller's magic was strictly sleight-of-hand (for Uri's chart, see Figure 9). Geller's principal mentor was Dr. Andrija Puharich, who arranged for Uri to be brought to the United States for testing at the Stanford Research Institute. Dr. Puharich had earlier been involved in testing the psychic surgery of the Brazilian healer Arigo (for Dr. Puharich's natal horoscope, see Figure 10). Then there was Franz Anton Mesmer, the 18th Century physician who healed the sick through hypnosis, which he called "animal magnetism" (see Mesmer's birth chart, Figure 11). Mesmer was scathingly denounced in his own time, but hypnosis is used as an adjunct to conventional medicine today. Other examples include occultist Aleister Crowley, alchemist/healer Allesandro di Cagliostro, Episcopalian minister-turned-spiritualist Bishop James Pike and California Governor Jerry Brown.

Chiron in the setting hemisphere inclines toward the individual who expects his or her mentor function to exhibit extremes of practicality and orderliness. The person born with this hemispheric emphasis of Chiron would tend to expect self-transformation to be a long and arduous road. By contrast, Chiron in the rising hemisphere inclines one to believe that self-transformation comes in an instantaneous flash of enlightenment. Of course the Chiron archetype as a whole holds more to a middle course between these two extremes — remember, we are dealing with a matter of emphasis on one of two opposites rather than a total exclusion of one or the other.

This Chiron placement tends to take on a Saturnian, as distinct from a Uranian, coloration. Self-transformation is viewed as a means

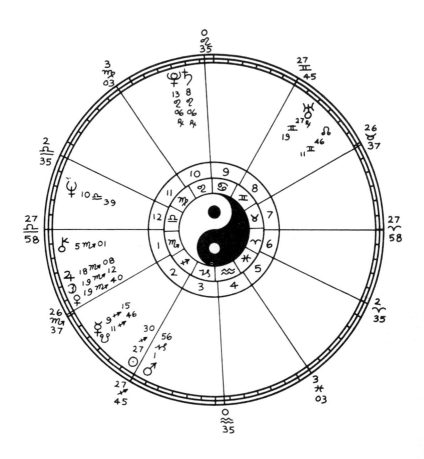

Figure 9. Natal horoscope (Tropical/Placidus) of Uri Geller, born
02:00 EET (00:00 UT), December 20, 1946, at Tel Aviv,
Israel (32N02, 34E49). Data source: From Geller to Nolle
via Puharich.

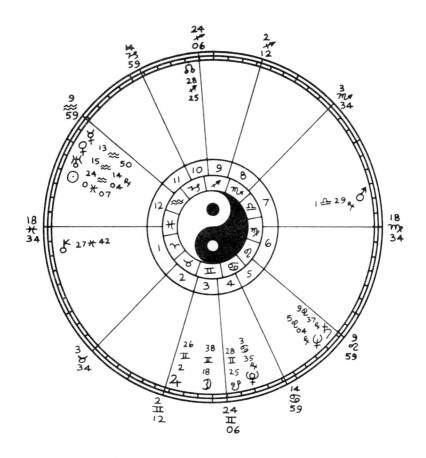

Figure 10. Natal horoscope (Tropical/Placidus) of Andrija Puharich, born 07:30 CST (13:30 UT), February 19, 1918, at Chicago, Illinois (41N53, 87W38). Data source: From Puharich to Nolle.

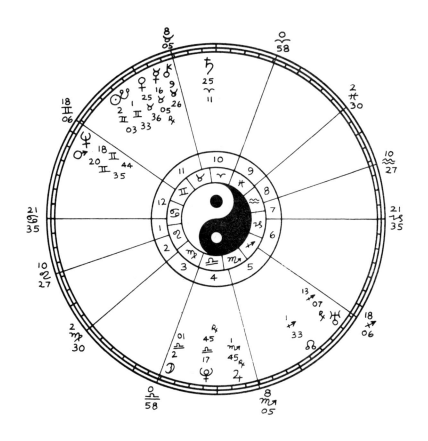

Figure 11. Natal horoscope (Tropical/Placidus) of Franz Anton Mesmer, born 08:00 LMT (07:12:04 UT), May 12, 1733, at Constance, Germany (43N45, 11E59). Data source: LMR, ABC.

to an ethical end, rather than an end in itself. Thus the individual may aim to transform himself or herself in order to help others somehow, or to find a mentor who preaches a doctrine something on the order of "By their works ye shall know them." Self-transformation may in fact be not enough for such a person, who might feel that the world itself must be transformed as part of the Quest. An illustrative characterization of the difference between the rising and setting hemisphere placements of Chiron, if I may borrow an example the late, great astrologer Marc Edmund Jones used in a more general context, is the distinction between ordering *à la carte* or *table d'hôte* respectively. In the first instance you pick and choose whatever strikes your fancy at the moment, while in the second case you select an already structured course. The former emphasis is intuitive and impulsive, the latter is cautious and conservative.

Examples of the right-hemisphere Chiron run the gamut from the sublime to the tragic. In the first category we find Dr. Albert Schweitzer, the theologian whose religious fervor could not be confined to the strictly spiritual. For Schweitzer, idealistic principles like faith and piety were not enough, so he took it upon himself to leave his native land and heal the sick in Africa. Schweitzer's chart is shown in Figure 12. Similar motives seem to have impelled the Reverend Jim Jones, whose miracle healings were legendary, to lead his flock to Jonestown, Guyana. However in Jones' case something went horribly wrong, and the Utopian community he aimed to create turned into a nightmarish massacre, an unspeakable atrocity that forever obliterated whatever good there may have been in the People's Temple (for Jones' chart, see Figure 13). Additional examples of right-hemisphere Chiron include all the Beatles except George Harrison, Marxist revolutionaries Angela Davis and Nicolai Lenin, reluctant terrorist Patricia Hearst, and feminist writers Germaine Greer and Gloria Steinem.

Cross-referencing the two sets of hemispheres — left, right, upper and lower, — gives rise to a further refinement of Chiron's basic orientation in the horoscope, resulting in four distinct focal zones. The lower left quadrant implies an expression of Chiron's function in a subjective, intuitive and highly personal way. Such an individual might be very poetic and either extremely charismatic or especially vulnerable to charismatic influence. He or she may be inclined to view self-transformation as a most mystical enterprise, a Quest of high metaphysical adventure. Solitude, all else being equal, would be a matter of great importance to this Seeker.

A prime example of this quadrant emphasis of Chiron is furnished by the natal horoscope of Dr. Elisabeth Kubler-Ross (see

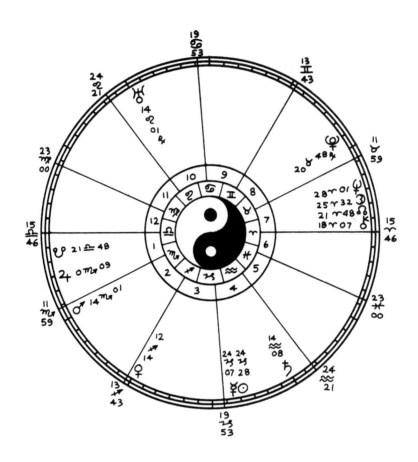

Figure 12. Natal horoscope (Tropical/Placidus) of Albert Schweitzer, born 23:50 LMT (23:20:56 UT), January 14, 1875, at Kayserburg, Alsace (48N09, 7E16). Data source: LMR, ABC.

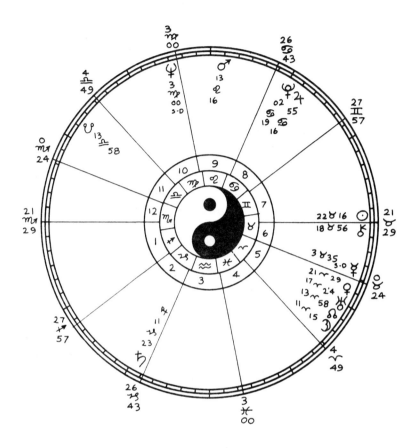

Figure 13. Natal horoscope (Tropical/Placidus) of Jim Jones, born
18:58 LMT (00:37:40 UT May 14), May 13, 1931, at Lynn,
Indiana (40N03, 84W55). Data source: Laurie Efrein,
"The Jonestown Tragedy", *CAO Times* Vol. 4 No. 1
(1979).

Figure 14). Dr. Kubler-Ross' work with terminal patients, reported in her book *On Death and Dying*, raises the possibility that the most private of all experiences — death — may be a truly liberating and beautiful rite of passage. Granted, any astrologer can see in Dr. Kubler-Ross' birth chart the signs of her preoccupation with death. She has, after all, a natal Sun-Pluto-North Node conjunction in the sign of the end of life, Cancer. And yet there is only one Planet in her chart which makes an immediate (less than two degrees orb) Ptolemaic aspect to the Moon, ruler of the sign Cancer. That Planet is Chiron, located in the lower left quadrant of the horoscope.

The lower right quadrant implies a Quest which is both private and methodical, a view of self-transformation in some ways akin to medieval alchemy — a matter of trial and error search for the right formula. One who is born with this Chiron emphasis would have high and rather inflexible standards by which to evaluate the Centaur Planet's function in his or her life. The Quest, the mentor, the holistic yearning for synthesis — all of these would be subjected to deep probing and constant critique. Emotional satisfaction coupled with logical consistency are the main criteria this individual uses to evaluate each step along the path of perosnal metamorphosis.

Feminist writer Germaine Greer exemplifies the lower right quadrant placement of Chiron (for Greer's birth chart, see Figure 15). In her book, *The Female Eunuch* (published in 1970, the year of Chiron's most recent aphelion), Greer convincingly argues that women can experience personal fulfillment only by renouncing the passive role foisted on them by a male-dominated culture. She hit upon this equation of linking emotional satisfaction (personal fulfillment) and logical consistency (renouncing the sexist double standard) only after a trial-and-error career that included acting and pornographic journalism.

The upper right quadrant position of Chiron inclines one to expect that transformation will come through following a set of procedures established by some external source, particularly a personal mentor or guru figure. Social recognition is important as a criterion by which to judge personal metamorphosis for this individual. "If no one else recognizes it, it can't be real," could be a rule of thumb for this Seeker. The object of the Quest for this person generally has a focus that is practical as well as social — some sort of objective change in the lives of others is sought by the native of Chiron in this quadrant.

Friedrich Engels, co-author (with Karl Marx, of course) of the *Communist Manifesto*, serves as a representative example of the upper right quadrant Chiron native (see Engels' birth chart, Figure

54

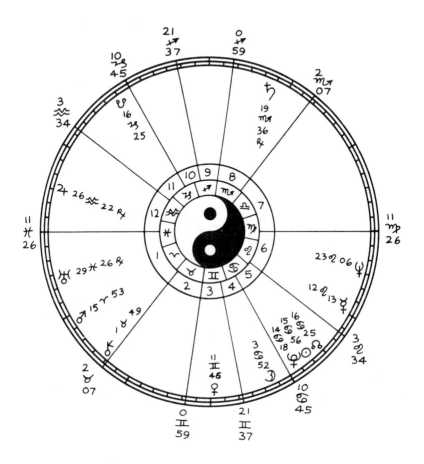

Figure 14. Natal horoscope (Tropical/Placidus) of Elisabeth Kubler-
Ross, born 22:45 MET (21:45 UT), July 8, 1926, at Zurich,
Switzerland (47N23, 8E32). Data source: June, 1982 Er-
rata to Lois M. Rodden, *Profiles of Women*. Tempe, AZ:
American Federation of Astrologers, 1979. (This source
hereafter designated LMR, POW.)

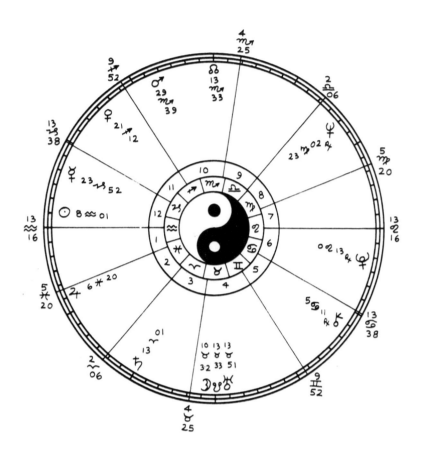

Figure 15. Natal horoscope (Tropical/Placidus) of Germaine Greer,
born 06:00 Zone 10 (20:00 UT), January 29, 1939 at Mel-
bourne, Australia (37S49, 144E58). Data source: LMR,
POW.

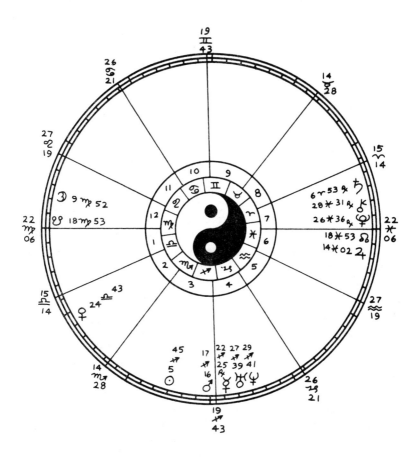

Figure 16. Natal horoscope (Tropical/Placidus) of Friedrich Engels,
born 00:48 LMT (00:19:08 UT), November 28, 1820, at
Barmen, Germany (51N17, 7E13). Data source: LMR,
ABC.

16). Engels freely acknowledged Karl Marx as his mentor in the development of communist political theory. Unlike all previous political theories, however, the communism of Marx and Engels was not merely descriptive, but transformative, having as its aim the revolutionary creation of a new social order. The great power of communist doctrine (foreshadowed in the T-Square complex in Engels' birth chart, involving the Ascendant, Uranus-Neptune conjunction and Pluto-Chiron conjunction) is indisputable — for better or worse, it has dominated the course of world history since its formulation shortly after the 1845 Chiron perihelion.

The upper left quadrant Chiron emphasis signifies one for whom self-tranformation is ultimately an idealistic searching for some person, environment or doctrine to act as a catalyst in the Quest. Intuition counts for more than logic in the mind of this Seeker, who feels that the alchemical key to personal metamorphosis is revealed in a flash of mystical enlightenment rather than through a step-by-step process of deduction. Often this Seeker is compelled by a metaphysical sense of restlessness to wander far and wide in pursuit of his or her own personal vision.

An excellent example of this quadrant emphasis of Chiron is afforded by the natal horoscope of Madame Helena Petrovna Blavatsky, founder of the Theosophical Society and author of *Isis Revealed* and *The Secret Doctrine* (see Blavatsky's chart, Figure 17). Blavatsky was a complex and controversial figure, a feminist, revolutionary, psychic and world traveler. She claimed to have spent time in Tibet, and to have come into contact there with the "mahatmas," avatars who initiated her into esoteric lore. Through her monumental books and her establishment (with Henry Steel Olcott) of the Theosophical Society, Madame Blavatsky has had a great impact on Seekers throughout the world. Although she projected her mentor-function outward onto the mahatmas of Tibetan lore, she remains to this day a mentor to millions of people.

Quadrant emphasis is one four-fold way of characterizing Chiron's placement in the natal horoscope, based on the interplay of two sets of dichotomies — above (heavenly), below (earth), rising (left) and setting (right). Another useful tetrarchical schema derives from the four elements of astrology. The twelve zodiacal signs are traditionally divided into four groups of three, each group consisting of signs belonging to the same element. The fire signs are Aries, Leo and Sagittarius. The earth signs are Taurus, Virgo and Capricorn. The water signs are Cancer, Scorpio and Pisces. And the air signs are Gemini, Libra and Aquarius.

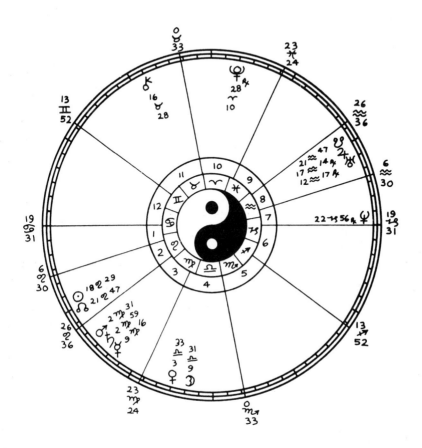

Figure 17. Natal horoscope (Tropical/Placidus) of Helena P. Blavatsky, born 02:17 LMT (23:56:56 UT August 11), August 12, 1831, at Ekaterinoslav, Russia (48N27, 35E01). Data source: LMR, POW.

Each of the four elements corresponds with a distinctive orientation to life, a unique personal style. In ancient and medieval times these four types were called humors; in more recent years they were revived by Carl Jung, who referred to them as preferred modes of functioning. The fire element is equivalent to the choleric humor of the ancients and to what Jung called the thinking type. An emphasis on the fire element in a horoscope signifies that the individual understands life as an act of will, a battle of wits. He or she lives according to principle, and views time as a logically-connected linear sequence of events, in which past, present and future are all causally related. One who is born with Chiron in a fire sign approaches the Quest as a supreme act of will, believing that self-transformation is a moral imperative that will sooner or later yield its secrets to the determined Seeker. Independence is highly valued by natives of the fire sign Chiron, for whom self-sufficiency is an essential part of the Quest. They are not easily influenced by external mentors directly, but can be convinced one way or the other by a well-presented, logical argument.

A sterling example of the fire sign Chiron is America's foremost atheist, Madalyn Murray O'Hair (see O'Hair's birth chart, Figure 18). With six Planets (including Chiron) and the Moon's North Node in fire signs, O'Hair's penchant for independence led her not only to reject the notion of a Supreme Being, but further to fight for the banning of prayer in public schools. It was a battle of wits that saw O'Hair, herself an attorney, arguing her case before the Supreme Court — and winning it, too. O'Hair's personal Quest took the form of a crusade against what she considered a great injustice. Her triumph is a tribute to her personally, as well as to the symbolic impact of the fire sign Chiron.

The earth element is analogous to what the ancient alchemists and philosophers called the bilious or melancholy humor; in Jung's typology, this element corresponds to the sensation category. Emphasis on the earth element in a horoscope suggests one who lives strictly for the present moment, without caring so much for past precedent or future promise. The individual born with Chiron in an earth sign tends to regard self-transformation not so much as an end in itself, but as a means for accomplishing some immediate and practical goal. For this kind of person, the pursuit of a desired goal is understood as requiring a personal metamorphosis on a very real and concrete level.

Dr. Martin Luther King, Jr., one of the greatest Americans of the 20th Century, is a paragon of the earth sign Chiron (for King's chart, see Figure 19). With four Planets (including Chiron), the

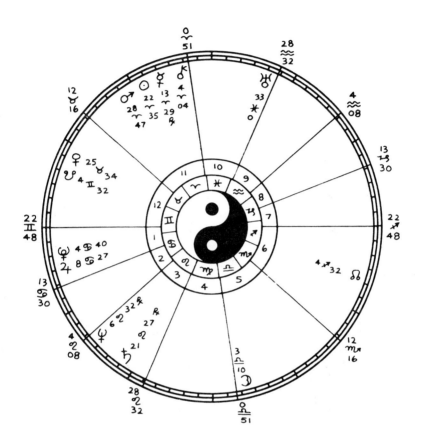

Figure 18. Natal horoscope (Tropical/Placidus) of Madalyn Murray O'Hair, born 09:00 EST (14:00 UT), April 13, 1919, at Pittsburgh, Pennsylvania (40N26, 80W01). Data source: LMR, POW.

61

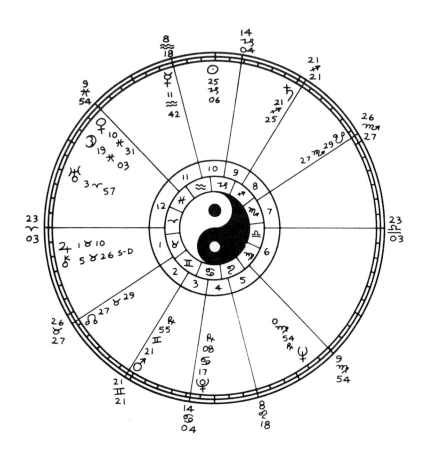

Figure 19. Natal horoscope (Tropical/Placidus) of Martin Luther King, Jr., born 11:00 CST (17:00 UT), January 15, 1929, at Atlanta, Georgia (33N45, 84W23). Data source: LMR, ABC.

Moon's Node and Midheaven in earth signs, Dr. King gently turned aside all criticism of the nonviolent black civil rights movement he led in the 1950's and '60's. Detractors of the movement feared that Dr. King's followers lacked patience in their press for reforms, but King pointed out that they had been patient for three centuries. Black radicals cried out for a bloody revolution, but Dr. King refused to stoop to the level of a "Bull" Connor. Instead he led a nonviolent campaign which instilled, pride, love and courage among his followers, won the hearts of his critics, and put his enemies to shame. Americans, both black and white, were transformed as a result of Dr. King's work, to such an extent that not even an assassin's bullet could put an end to the dream of racial equality.

The air element parallels the sanguinary humor of alchemy and the intuitive type in Jung's system of psychological classification. When this element predominates in the birth chart of an individual, he or she is always looking beyond immediate circumstances, anticipating another time or place which, although it is not present here and now, may soon be. Others may interpret this as a sign of idealism (or worse, flightiness), but for the individual himself or herself it is simply a matter of the here and now never being sufficient to satisfy. An air sign Chiron points to one who is restless with the constraints of the present and eager to initiate a process which will ultimately bring some worthy ideal out of the realm of fantasy and down into the real world. Self-transformation for such an individual tends to be matter of mind control, of changing the way the world is perceived rather than changing the world per se.

An outstanding example of the air sign Chiron is Annie Besant, a multi-faceted social reformer and president of the Theosophical Society in India from 1907 until her death in 1933 (for Besant's chart, see Figure 20). An ardent feminist, Besant was once arrested for dispensing information on birth control — in 1877! In addition to equal rights for women, she also fought on behalf of the labor movement, intellectual freedom and home rule for India and Ireland. When her lover, George Bernard Shaw, introduced Annie Besant to the literature of Theosophy, she converted from atheism, eventually assuming the presidency of the Theosophical Society upon the death of Henry Steel Olcott in 1907. Always standing with one foot in this world and the other in some next or transcendantal world, Besant fully expressed the multifarious potential represented by Chiron in the air signs.

The water element is equivalent to what the alchemists of old called the phlegmatic humor. In Jung's schematic, it corresponds to the feeling type. An emphasis on the water element in a horoscope

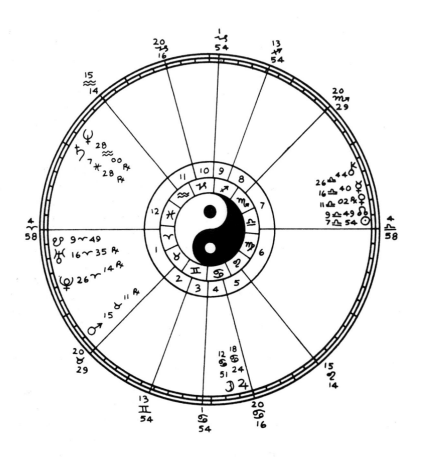

Figure 20. Natal horoscope (Tropical/Placidus) of Annie Besant, born 17:29 LMT (17:29:24 UT), October 1, 1847, at London, England (51N31, 0W06). Data source: LMR, POW.

is symbolic of an individual who responds to life primarily in terms of emotion. This sort of person tends to live in the past, which has already been given a secure emotional value. He or she more often than not is doubtful, even apprehensive, of the present and future. Natives of the water sign Chiron are inclined to regard self-transformation as a most mystical Quest, replete with occult drama and ritual. Traditional forms of mysticism can play an important role in the personal metamorphosis of this type of individual. Feelings for other people, whether positive or negative, are crucial determinants of the life mission for this Seeker.

Dr. Jonas Salk, the heroic physician who banished polio from Planet Earth, illustrates well some of the characteristics of this Chiron emphasis (see Salk's natal horoscope, Figure 21). With seven Planets (including Chiron) and the Moon's North Node in water signs, Dr. Salk put an end to the fearful reign of a cruel, crippling disease. Few people today remember that, prior to 1955, summer was polio season, when seasonal outbreaks of the dread disease would strike down thousands of innocent victims. One of those victims, after he became President, inspired Americans with his famous pronouncement, "The only thing we have to fear is fear itself." More to the point, as far as Jonas Salk is concerned, President Franklin Roosevelt founded the National Foundation for Infantile Paralysis. A generous grant from the National Foundation materially aided Dr. Salk's research, which eventually resulted in a safe and effective polio vaccine. It was for Salk an emotionally-charged twelve-year Quest, fraught with controversy (including scare campaigns directed against his vaccine), that finally culminated on April 12, 1955, with the announcement that field trials have proven the safety and effectiveness of the Salk vaccine. Born from a desire to relieve human suffering, Jonas Salk's life work was made possible through the generosity of a famous polio victim from out of the past, and resulted in a brighter future for all humankind.

The four elements are one way of dividing the zodiacal signs to reveal significant differences in basic orientation. Another equally valid rationale distinguishes three major categories of signs according to what is called their quality. Quality in this case has no connotation of better or worse; rather it refers to varying dispositions with regard to change or action. The four cardinal signs, Aries, Cancer, Libra and Capricorn, are the opening signs of the four seasons. The fixed signs, Taurus, Leo, Scorpio and Aquarius, correspond to the middle of each season. The mutable signs, Gemini, Virgo, Sagittarius and Pisces, are the closing signs of the four seasons. Each quality has a unique character analogous to the Holy Trinity of Hin-

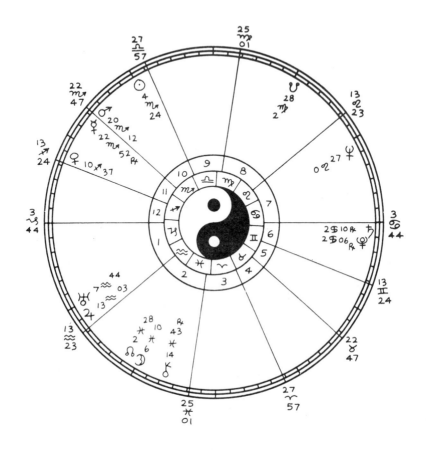

Figure 21. Natal horoscope (Tropical/Placidus) of Jonas Salk, born
11:15 EST (16:15 UT), October 28, 1914, at New York,
New York (40N42, 74W00). Data source: LMR, ABC.

duism: Brahma the Creator (cardinal), Vishnu the Preserver (fixed), and Shiva the Destroyer-Restorer (mutable).

A horoscopic emphasis on cardinal signs generally suggests that the individual is apt to be an initiator (in the metaphysical as well as the ordinary sense of the word), one who independently sets out on a new course — all the while with the intention of motivating others to follow. With Chiron occupying a cardinal sign in the birth chart, one tends to pursue an intensely individual Quest. Others are apt to sense the unique character of such a path, adopt it as their own, and then insist on casting the originator in a guru or mentor role.

Mohandas K. (Mahatma) Gandhi, with four Planets (including Chiron), the Ascendant and Midheaven in cardinal signs, is an archetype of the Cardinal Chiron. There have been many revolutionaries before and since Gandhi, but he was the first and so far the only one to successfully combine revolution with nonviolence. The ideal of nonviolence of course had a long history before Gandhi came on the scene, having antecedents in both Hindu and Christian tradition. Gandhi put nonviolence into practice as a revolutionary political force, restoring the spiritual identity of the Hindu people even as he overthrew their colonial masters. Spiritually as well as politically, Gandhi set India free, without firing a shot. It is an example many revolutionaries have since been inspired to emulate, a standard very few have been able to maintain (see Gandhi's natal horoscope, Figure 22).

A fixed sign preponderance in the birth chart is symbolic of one who follows an established course with great intensity, often surpassing in some respects the person who originated that course of action in the first place. Those born with Chiron in one of the fixed signs more than make up in concentration what they may lack in originality. They tend to adopt a plan for self-transformation which has been handed down from some exemplary person who fills the role of guru or mentor. Through dedication, courage and tenacity, the fixed sign Chiron native can reach and even transcend his or her objective, giving concrete form to what began only as an intellectual or emotional impulse.

The birth chart of Martin Luther King, Jr. (refer to Figure 19), especially in view of its connection to Mahatma Gandhi, is a good example of the fixed sign Chiron. The horoscopes of these two men are rather like mirror images. Gandhi's Rising Sign sits on King's Descendant, and vice versa; both charts feature Jupiter in Taurus and Saturn in Sagittarius; and each man was born under a square aspect from Moon to Mars. Gandhi's style of nonviolent revolution

67

Figure 22. Natal horoscope (Tropical/Placidus) of Mohandas K. Gandhi, born 07:11:48 LMT (02:33:20 UT), October 2, 1869, at Porbandar, India (21N38, 69E37). Data source: LMR, ABC.

was consciously adopted by King, with much the same result, in that the revolution was both politically successful and a redeeming experience for all concerned. Martin Luther King's use of nonviolent revolution obviously owes much to his spiritual/political mentor, Gandhi, and yet King in some respects surpassed his guru. The civil rights movement, after all, succeeded in the very heartland of racist oppression, whereas Gandhi's revolution owed its success in no small measure to the fact that the oppressors were thousands of miles away (even though their henchmen were very much right on the scene). In the end, mentor and protege met the same fate: King, as Gandhi had been before him, was assassinated by a bigot with a gun.

A mutable sign emphasis in the birth chart signifies one who finishes things, rather than originating or sustaining them. This type is a transitional figure, who prepares the way for new forms of thought and action. When Chiron tenants one of the mutable signs in the birth chart, the individual may pursue personal metamorphosis indirectly, with some other objective in mind. Yet self-transformation can occur just the same, even when it is not specifically what the person aims to achieve. Often, the kind of fundamental transmutation that takes place is the result of destroying self-limiting concepts of identity. The individual as a rule does not consciously intend for this to happen, but once it comes to pass he or she may feel that some subconscious force or superconscious Guide was all along interceding to bring it about. Paradox is central to the archetypal significance of this Seeker, who promotes crisis as the prelude to creation, destruction as the prerequisite to a new birth.

An appropriately paradoxical exemplar of the Mutable Chiron is furnished by the birth chart of Karl Marx (see Figure 23). Although Marx is generally considered the Father of modern communism, the political movement that bears his name is original neither in theory nor in practice. Theoretically, Marxism is nothing more than a blend of Hegelian dialectic and extreme labor unionism — neither of these did Marx invent. And in political reality there is no such thing as a dictatorship of the proletariat anywhere in the countries where Marxism is law — there is a proletariat and a dictatorship, to be sure, but they are two completely distinct phenomena. Marx's intent was to make possible a world of political equity; instead, his doctrine has given birth to one of the more tyrannical oligarchies in planetary history. With his six Planets (including Chiron) and Midheaven in mutable signs, Karl Marx apparently believed that communism would prove itself the last best hope of humankind, and that history would inevitably pull the whole world

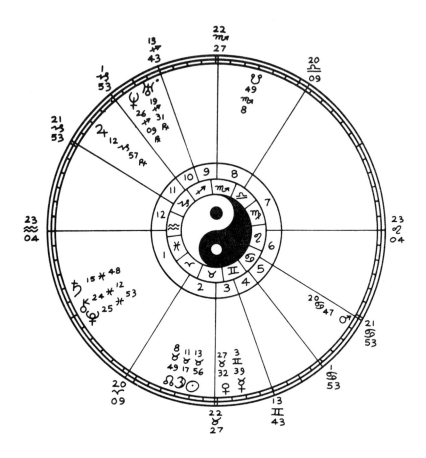

Figure 23. Natal horoscope (Tropical/Placidus) of Karl Marx, born 02:00 LMT (01:35:36 UT), May 5, 1818, at Trier, Germany (49N45, 6E06). Data source: LMR, ABC.

into the communist camp. The irony is that anyone could believe, as Marx did, that human salvation could come out of a theory which reduces human beings to the level of cogs in an economic machine: The very same flaw he so deplored in the capitalist system, Marx ironically made the cornerstone of communism.

Finally in our survey of fundamental Chiron categories we come to a consideration of the direction of this Minor Planet's apparent motion. From the (geocentric) perspective of a terrestrial observer, normal Planetary motion follows the counterclockwise direction of the zodiac, and is called direct. Motion in the reverse direction is called retrograde (abbreviated R_x). With the exception of Sun and Moon, which are always direct, all Planets are retrograde a greater or lesser minority of the time. Pluto is retrograde more often than any other Planet, and Venus less often, while Chiron falls between these two extremes. However even Pluto, the retrograde champ, is direct in motion about 56 percent of the time, so retrogression is always the exception rather than the rule. At the moment of beginning retrograde motion, and again at the moment ending retrograde to resume direct motion, a Planet appears to be stationary in the heavens. The retrograde station (abbreviated SR_x, meaning stationary-about-to-go-retrograde) and the direct station (abbreviated SD, meaning stationary-about-to-go-direct) are always very brief, and consequently it is rather rare to find a birth chart which features any Planet either stationary-retrograde or stationary-direct. In descending order of rarity, the two stations are equal in duration and by far the rarest, followed by retrograde motion and then finally by direct motion which is the normal state.

A Planet in direct motion, being the prevalent situation over the long run, represents neither more nor less than the normal archetypal function of that Planet. Retrograde motion, being less common in comparison, puts a special emphasis on a given Planetary function. Both stations, because they are so very rare, heighten the emphasis on a Planet's function to an extreme level. None of these several states of apparent motion in any way changes the fundamental archetype of a Planet, it should be emphasized. Whether stationary, retrograde or direct in motion, Chiron remains Chiron, Mercury remains Mercury, etc. All that changes is a matter of emphasis on the Planetary function in question.

As with all Planets from Jupiter on outward to the limits of the known solar system, Chiron direct is not significantly more emphasized in the birth chart than Chiron retrograde. This is because, in the long run, Chiron appears to move direct only 50 percent more than retrograde, in the proportion:

$$D: R_x = 3:2.$$

What difference in emphasis there is is subtle. Generally speaking, Chiron direct in an individual's birth chart points to one for whom the mentor and the Quest are matters of immediate concern, to be experienced through direct action. In contrast, Chiron retrograde inclines more toward the person for whom these functions are mediated, removed from direct action by the interference of contemplation. In a word, the native of Chiron retrograde is more occupied with *thinking* about self-transformation than is the native of Chiron direct.

The terms sublimation and repression are often used to describe the quality of a retrograde Planet's function, and there is some justification for this practice. However it is important to keep in mind that a function sublimated or repressed does not cease to exist, nor does it become any less important — rather, the reverse is generally true. Because Chiron is an archetype which operates mainly on the subconscious and superconscious levels, retrograde Chiron (be it sublimated or repressed or whatever label you prefer) is not Chiron denied. In truth, the more one attempts to repress the need for self-transoformation, the more it keeps coming to mind — if only in terms of enigmatic dreams and other, similar experiences.

There are a number of examples of Chiron retrograde and direct in the twenty-one sample horoscopes considered in this chapter. In the former category we have medical researcher Jonas Salk, communist writer Friedrich Engels, fantasy writer Carlos Castaneda, feminist Germaine Greer and political guru Mahatma Gandhi. Examples of Chiron in direct motion are exhibited by the birth charts of social reformer/Theosophist Annie Besant, Theosophy cofounder H.P. Blavatsky, musicians Bob Dylan and John Lennon, psychologists Elisabeth Kubler-Ross, Carl Jung and Sigmund Freud, writer Hermann Hesse, communist Karl Marx, physicians Andrija Puharich, Albert Schweitzer and Franz Anton Mesmer (all of whom are noted for their multiple interests), psychic Uri Geller, atheist Madalyn Murray O'Hair and cultist Jim Jones.

A stationary Planet, whether SR_x or SD, changes everything. Because stations are so relatively rare in proportion to retrograde or direct motion, they may be said to represent a tremendous intensification of a Planetary archetype. The Planet's function remains the same, of course, but its overall importance in the individual's life is greatly emphasized, to the point that it assumes a more-than-personal (even historical!) meaning. Thus stationary Chiron may signify one whose personal Quest can become a mass crusade, or one whose own self-transformation ends up transforming many others as well. Chiron is always a key personal archetype in any birth chart, but when stationary the Centaur Planet is potentially dramatized to the level of a crucial social or historical archetype.

Examples of stationary Chiron are relatively rare. Of the twenty-one individuals whose birth charts are presented in this chapter, only one person was born on the exact day of a Chiron station. That person is Martin Luther King, Jr., the nonviolent social reformer who is certain to go down in history as one of the most influential Americans of the 20th Century (refer to King's natal horoscope, Figure 19). There can be no better example of one whose personal Quest was so dynamic that millions of people were caught up in its fulfillment.

CHAPTER 6

SIGN OF THE CENTAUR CHIEF

What's your sign? It's a question more than 80 percent of America's adult population can readily answer. Granted, nearly all who do answer will do so in terms of Sun signs. There are twelve of these of course, each being in effect for approximately thirty days every year. Sun signs are by far the most popular dimension of astrology. In fact they are so well known as to obscure the fact that the same twelve signs normally thought of in connection with the solar calendar also apply to celestial bodies other than the Sun. The general public as a rule has no inkling of the diversity astrologers and their students take for granted; namely (to say the least) that the signs of the zodiac are relevant not only to the Sun, but also to the Moon and all the other Planets as well.

The reason for the popularity of Sun signs is no mystery. They are popular because they are very easy to determine. All you have to do is remember that Sun signs start with Aries around March 21 (specifically at the moment of vernal equinox), and continue in sequence with each successive sign beginning around the 21st of each succeeding month. To be sure there are minor complications, arising from the fact that Sol may change signs a few days before or after the 21st of a given month, but by and large most people seldom need even glance at a calendar to determine the Sun sign in effect at any particular time.

When it comes to other Planetary signs, the simplicity of Sun sign astrology is nowhere in evidence. Moon signs, for example, change every two or three days. Mercury and Venus signs pay no attention to particular dates of the month, and outer Planets like Uranus, Neptune and Pluto can spend years in the same sign — so can Chiron, by the way. In order to determine such Planetary signs as these it is necessary to consult either a computer or an ephemeris

74

(a table of Planetary position), or a table that is derived from one of these two sources.

What's your Chiron sign? Fear not, Dear Reader, the answer is ready at hand. Simply locate your birth date in Appendix I, and you can tell at a glance which Sign Chiron occupied when you were born. Granted, there are some limitations to this table. For one thing it only goes back as far as 1890. I had to draw the line somewhere, and that's where I drew it! (Readers born before 1890 who wish to determine their Chiron Sign, please see Appendix II.) And then there is the matter of cusps, the dates when one sign ends or another begins. If you were born on one of the cusp dates listed in Appendix I, you will need to obtain a copy of your natal horoscope to ascertain which sign applies to you (see Appendix II).

Of course you can get ever so much more information by consulting a copy of your complete birth chart in the first place, because it tells not only Chiron's sign position but House position as well, in addition to the sign and house location of all the other Planets, not to mention a wealth of more detailed information. Astrologers and their students by definition already have access to their birth chart, even though Chiron may be excluded due to its relatively recent discovery. Readers who lack a copy of their natal horoscope, or whose chart does not include Chiron, are referred to Appendix II for further instructions. In the meantime nearly everyone can immediately determine his or her natal Chiron Sign through reference to the tables in Appendix I.

Astrologers and their students are likely to have a number of fundamental philosophical questions regarding Chiron Signs, questions that deserve consideration prior to any description of these sign archetypes per se. In a moment we'll discover what each Sign means, but for the present we really ought to give our inquiry a broader base. For instance, in reference to which zodiac shall Chiron's position be considered? There are after all two fundamentally different zodiacs recognized in the astrological community, the sidereal and the tropical.

The tropical zodiac, the option most widely preferred in the Western world today, divides the ecliptic circle (the apparent path of the Planets from a geocentric perspective) into twelve equal segments, beginning with Sol's apparent location at the moment of the vernal equinox (the first day of spring in the northern hemisphere). Sol's location at that instant marks the beginning of the sign Aries, and all the other signs follow in thirty degree increments from there on. The sidereal zodiac is an alternative division of the ecliptic circle, based not on the equinox but on the stars that lie along the ecliptic plane. Although still widely used in India, the sidereal zodiac has few proponents in the Western world at present. These two zodiacs allot the same names and sequence to their twelve sectors, but owing to the precession of the equinoxes they are out of phase with respect to each other nowadays. Thus tropical Aries presently is roughly equivalent to sidereal Pisces, tropical Taurus to sidereal Aries, tropical Gemini to sidereal Taurus, etc. For the purposes of this book, all references to signs are to be understood in the context of the tropical zodiac, not the sidereal.

Students of the cosmic art/science are accustomed to think of each sign as being "ruled" by a Planet, and of each Planet as "ruling" one or at most two signs. This is a technicality that goes back at least as far as Claudius Ptolemy (2nd Century C.E.), who considered Mars the ruler of Aries and Scorpio, Venus the ruler of Taurus and Libra, Mercury the ruler of Gemini and Virgo, Luna the ruler of Cancer, Sol the ruler of Leo, Jupiter the ruler of Sagittarius and Pisces, and Saturn the ruler of Capricorn and Aquarius. Ptolemy's notion of rulership is rooted in a concept of natural affinity. Thus, for example, since Venus is sensuous (like Taurus) and aesthetic (like Libra), it seemed only natural for this Planet to rule these two Signs. The Ptolemaic system of rulerships began to break down with the discovery of new Planets, starting with Uranus in 1781. At that time astrologers stripped Saturn of its dominion over Aquarius, assigning that sign to Uranus instead. Likewise Neptune eventually displaced Jupiter as ruler of Pisces, and Pluto replaced Mars as ruler of Scorpio.

The concept of Planets and Signs being associated through rulership quite naturally might lead astrology students to the question, which sign does Chiron rule? Candidates for the sign of Chiron's dominion might be Sagittarius, if only because the Sagittarian Centaur is none other than Chiron himself; or perhaps Scorpio, because this sign is associated with healing and death (two obvious elements of the Chiron myth); or perhaps Libra, in view of the Centaur Planet's function as a link between two opposites, a quality which is in some ways similar to Libra's traditional role as the sign of relationships. However, the whole question of which Planet rules which sign poses another, even more fundamental question; what is the meaning of Planetary rulership per se?

Planetary rulership of the zodiacal signs may have made some sense in an age when there were only seven known Planets, as was the case in Ptolemy's time. The problem then was how to allocate only seven Planets in relation to the twelve signs and twelve Houses. Horoscopes of that era were characterized by great empty spaces, and to tie them all together in one skein of relationship required that each Planet be given dominion over at least one sign. The problem was especially acute with regard to the houses. Seven Planets can occupy at most only seven houses, leaving nearly half the horoscope empty. Planetary rulership of the signs effectively solved this problem. Since all houses have a sign on their cusp, and since each sign had a Planetary ruler, the seven Planets could effectively activate every House in a horoscope. This served to fill the cosmic emptiness of the birth chart, bringing an apparently incomplete image into some kind of sensible focus.

Planetary rulership of the signs is really only an artificial scheme (albeit a useful and even natural one, in view of the affinities between certain signs and Planets) that has certainly outlived its usefulness. Today, if we count not only Chiron and the four principal asteroids (Ceres, Pallas, Juno and Vesta) but the several other Minor Planets which have some currency in the astrological community (e.g. Hidalgo, Icarus, Sappho, Eros and Toro), there are more than enough cosmic bodies to go around, and far too many to consistently apply any simplistic system of rulerships. The problem of filling out the horoscope and tying it all together is an obsolete dilemma, rendered superfluous by the bounty of our solar system. This is not meant to deny that particular Planets and signs share some common symbolic meanings, only to say that the traditional concept of rulership is an arbitrary, outmoded and foolishly absolute dogma. Consequently the question of Chiron's rulership over one sign or another is a moot point.

Finally in our preliminary consideration of Chiron signs, it is worth noting that, owing to the extreme elliptical orbit of the Centaur Planet, Chiron's stay in the various signs varies quite a bit. Because Chiron's perihelion occurs in the western extreme of the zodiac, and because any Planet's perihelion coincides with swift apparent motion, the Centaur Planet spends relatively little time in the Western signs. In contrast, Chiron's aphelion falls in the eastern extreme of the zodiac. Moving slowly here, Chiron takes a long time to pass through the Eastern signs. In concrete terms this means that Chiron spends a lot more of its approximate 50.3-year circuit through the zodiac in such Eastern signs as Pisces (7.94 years) and Aries (8.28 years) than in such Western signs as Virgo (1.78 years) and Libra (1.79 years). This remarkable pattern of Chiron sign distribution makes certain natal Chiron signs relatively rare, and others fairly common. In any complete orbital cycle of Chiron, for example, there are likely to be more people born with Chiron in Aries than with Chiron in Leo, Virgo, Libra and Scorpio combined.

Figure 24 illustrates the general pattern of Chiron sign distribution for the interval 1890 to 1999 (the time span covered in Appendix I). Seasoned astrology students may recognize this pattern as more or less a mirror image of the normal Rising Sign distribution for births in the north temperate latitudes. Figure 25 illustrates a typical rising sign distribution for north temperate latitude births. This particular array comes from a sample of 298 natal charts gathered in a survey of the readers of *Horoscope* magazine. Whereas the Chiron sign distribution tends to peak in the Eastern signs of the zodiac (viz. Capricorn, Aquarius, Pisces, Aries, Taurus and Gemini), the rising sign distribution (in north temperate latitudes at least) tends to peak in the Western signs (viz. Cancer, Leo, Virgo, Libra, Scorpio and Sagittarius).

Without going too deeply into the technicalities, the reason rising signs tend to peak in the Western signs and trough in the Eastern signs is that the former take more time and the latter less to cross the Ascendant. (This is true of the northern temperate latitudes. The further north one goes from the equator, the more pronounced is the preponderance of Western rising signs.) The preponderance of Western rising signs in the temperate latitudes symbolically reflects the type of human nature necessary for the high degree of socialization that is so characteristic of the civilization prevailing in these latitudes. Because a majority of the individuals living in this civilization have rising signs of the Western, relationship-oriented variety, they are predisposed to the socialization process to a much greater extent than natives of the equatorial region.

Figure 26 compares the time each sign takes to cross the Ascendant at the equator and at 60 degrees North latitude. The relatively homogenous distribution of rising signs at the equator, as compared to the distinctive array farther north, coincides with a generally less socialized culture in the more southerly region. The form of culture which even today prevails in the equatorial regions is virtually tribal, with very little specialization of social and cultural roles. In contrast, specialization is the chief characteristic of culture in the temperate zones. By its very nature, specialization both creates and depends on interdependence, hence giving rise to the high degree of socialization that is so characteristic of the high technology civilization in the temperate zones of Planet Earth. If it is true, as astrological tradition by and large maintains, that human beings project their personality mainly in terms of the rising sign, then the relationship of rising sign distribution to cultural patterns in the temperate and equatorial regions takes on an especially revealing aspect.

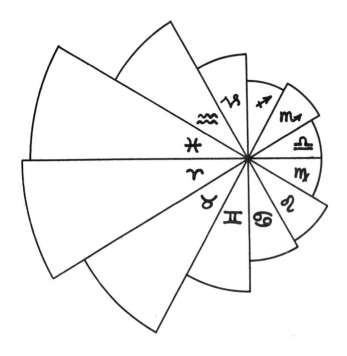

Figure 24. Chiron sign distribution (Tropical) 1890-1999.

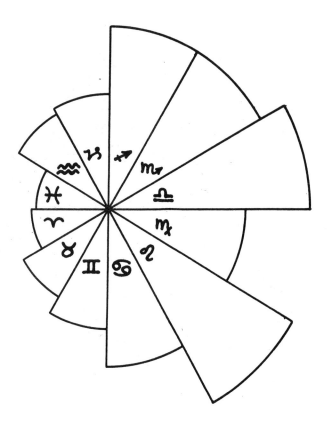

Figure 25. Rising sign distribution (Tropical/Placidus) (from sample of 298 *Horoscope* magazine readers' birth charts, having a median birth latitude of 41 degrees north).

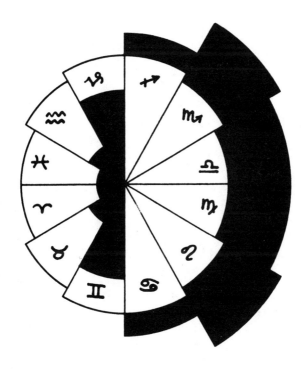

Figure 26. Rising sign time distribution at equator (white sectors) and 60 degrees North latitude (black sectors). (Tropical/Placidus).

Chiron sign distribution, in contrast to rising signs, downplays the Western, relationship-oriented sector of the zodiac in favor of the Eastern, individualistic sector. Both are natural patterns, and yet each is radically different in orientation. Chiron's emphasis on the individualistic signs parallels the Chief Centaur's mythical role as a mentor to heroes, a Quest Guide. The Quest, the heroic labor that is possible for each of us, has as its aim the full self-realization of the individual. While anyone's personal Quest may have social or cultural ramifications, it is first and foremost a process of individuation, having as its primary goal the fulfillment of the individual's dharma or life mission. The predominance in any human population of individuals whose natal horoscopes are characterized by Chiron in the Eastern signs is a process of natural selection binding Heaven and Earth in one holistic tapestry of meaning and function. It is a celestial reminder of Chiron's central role in the evolution of the individual.

Chiron's natural predilection for the Eastern signs points out another of the Centaur Planet's attributes; namely its function as a maverick or loner. Any hero by definition must stand virtually alone, at least at some critical moment, against the stacked deck of karma (fate). But at the same time we must not forget that Chiron symbolizes wholeness, the synthetic reconciliation of thesis and antithesis. In this respect the relative scarcity of Chiron in the Western signs puts special emphasis on the individual whose birth chart features the Centaur Planet in one of these sectors of the zodiac. Being the exceptions to a general pattern of distribution, these people are figuratively singled out by a process of natural selection. Because Chiron in one of the Western signs (e.g. Libra) is so rare, relatively speaking, the individual whose birth chart is so characterized is singled out, as it were, for a special role. This person's Quest will still be a process of individuation, of course, but it will be carried out in terms of a special relationship to other people.

Theoretical considerations and overall patterns of distribution aside, it's time for a closer look at your own Chiron sign, Dear Reader. However as we proceed you must remember that Chiron's sign position alone is not the end-all and be-all of anyone's birth chart, any more than any other astrological function by itself can represent the whole person.

Every one of us is a unique individual, each one a whole complex of meaning. To isolate any component of this whole is artificial and misleading by definition, unless we realize from the outset that such a procedure is merely provisional and always subject to further refinement in light of the broader perspective as it emerges. To approach the whole chart as a thing-in-itself complete is for most people a mind-boggling prospect, especially when (as is the case with Chiron) certain functional concentrations of meaning subsisting in the whole are unknown or unfamiliar. The way out of this impasse requires a compromise of consciousness, a suspension of judgement combined with an openness to possibilities for significant symbols. The trick, if one can call it that, is to gather individual threads of the personal Chiron archetype with an eye toward weaving these threads into a tapestry of meaning that stands for the whole person. Chiron's hemispheric position in the birth chart, its quadrant location, its element and quality, and its kind of motion (whether stationary, retrograde or direct) are some of the many threads that go to make up one's personal tapestry. So too is Chiron's sign. Therefore as we proceed, remember that what is said about your Chiron sign is intended only as a mere outline, to be filled in and expanded according to the dictates of your own wisdom and experience.

CHIRON IN ARIES

In many respects these people are trailblazers, pioneers and/or mavericks. They are oriented toward anticipating the shape of things to come, and seek to lead the world (kicking and screaming, if need be) into tomorrow. Their most influential mentors are people who can show them how to establish an independent course and stick to it. Crucial learning experiences for Chiron in Aries natives are often found at the frontiers of social, cultural, artistic or intellectual change. When the old rules are breaking down, these people will be ready with a new plan.

The search for identity is a paramount issue in the lives of persons born under this Chiron sign, who can conceive of nothing more important than self realization. Merely to know who one is cannot be enough for these people, who will not be satisfied with anything less than the fulfillment of all their personal potentials. They want to be more and to do more, to search out the limits of self and then go beyond those limits.

Examples of Chiron in Aries include psychedelic advocate (and lately a spokesman for outer space colonization) Timothy Leary, President Jimmy Carter, Canadian Prime Minister Pierre Trudeau, writers Jack Anderson, Isaac Asimov, William Buckley, Carlos Castaneda, Jack Kerouac and Kurt Vonnegut, occultists Sybil Leek and Aleister Crowley, humanitarian physicians Albert Schweitzer and Tom Dooley, educator Maria Montessori and psychologist Carl Jung. All of these people are remembered or are presently celebrated as pioneers in one sense of the word or another, and any one of them would be an excellent illustration of Chiron in Aries. Take Kurt Vonnegut, for instance (for his birth chart, see Figure 27).

Because of his innovative approach to science fiction writing, Vonnegut achieved a cult-figure status in the 1970's. While most writers who specialize in this genre merely explore alternative realities in an entertaining way, Vonnegut goes beyond this level of exposition. His novels explore the absurdity of the human condition in a way that rivals such existentialist writers as Sartre, Kafka and Camus. Vonnegut's natal four-Planet T-Square pattern (Moon in Leo in the eighth house, Mercury and Jupiter conjunct in Scorpio in the eleventh, Mars in Aquarius in the second) suggests a keen insight into human conflict and relationship. With the addition of Chiron to the chart another T-Square is revealed, Saturn in Libra in the tenth house opposing Chiron in Aries in the fourth house, both squared by Pluto in Cancer at the eighth cusp: This is the pattern that brings Vonnegut into focus as an artist who captures the verities of human experience, who sees the future in the present while fondly remembering the past.

Vonnegut was an eyewitness to the Allied bombing of Dresden, where he was a captive POW at the time. The attack, which killed 60,000 people or more, took place on February 13-14, 1945, and it created a firestorm visible as much as 200 miles away. That hellish experience seems to have been a key moment in Vonnegut's personal Quest — it is central to his novel *Slaughterhouse-Five*. The Dresden attack coincided with a progressed Mercury-Uranus square for Vonnegut, an unmistakable portent of a radical upheaval (Uranus) in awareness (Mercury).

Progressions, in case you are unfamiliar with the term, are a means of studying the unfoldment of a particular horoscope through time. In the common day-for-a-year measure, a chart is advanced one day for each year after birth. As Vonnegut was 22 years old at the time of the Dresden attack, his progressed horoscope for that event is calculated for 22 days after his birthdate. His experience of the Dresden bombing seems to have played a crucial role in Vonnegut's psyche, making him keenly aware of the tragically absurd frailties to which homo sapiens is subject. (Dresden, military historians say, was bombed mainly because it had not been bombed before. Can you think of a more inscrutable reason to kill 60,000 people, most of them civilians?) At any rate it was not until 1952, the year that Jupiter in the heavens came to the degree of Chiron in Vonnegut's natal horoscope, that his existential anguish brought forth Vonnegut's first novel, *Player Piano*. In *Slaughterhouse-Five* (his highly-acclaimed

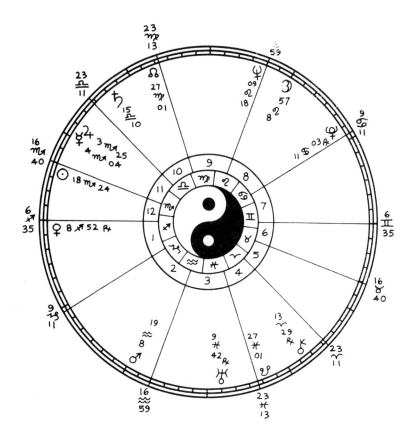

Figure 27. Natal horoscope (Tropical/Placidus) of Kurt Vonnegut,
born 08:00 CST (14:00 UT), November 11, 1922, at In-
dianapolis, Indiana (39N46, 86W90). Data source: LMR,
ABC.

1969 novel), the main character (Billy Pilgrim) is in some respects an autobiographical analog for Vonnegut himself. Significantly, Billy Pilgrim discovers, in 1967, that linear time is an illusion. 1967, it turns out, was the year that Vonnegut's natally retrograde Chiron turned direct by progression.

CHIRON IN TAURUS

For many people value is something measured in money, but value means much more than that for natives of Chiron in Taurus. They understand that things have value only to the extent that people value them, that value is a state of mind rather than a price tag. Those who are born under Chiron in Taurus are fundamentally concerned with the concept of value both abstractly and concretely. To learn what they want and what they are willing to live with (both psychologically and materially) is a key issue in their lives. Their mentors appear in the guise of individuals who place a value judgement on some phase of human experience. The Chiron in Taurus native responds to his or her mentor by attempting to enforce the mentor's value judgements as far as possible — and sometimes this can be a very, very long way.

To want something enough to secure and preserve it is a keynote in the lives of these people, who can triumph despite terrific odds because for them defeat would mean a denial of selfhood. While they are seldom true innovators, these people have a way of picking up someone else's torch and then carrying it so well and so far that they make us forget their predecessors. They have the ability to translate the abstract and theoretical into concrete and practical terms. For them, the Quest is an act of self-transformation that aims to transform not only the self, but the environment as well.

Examples of the Chiron in Taurus native include Cuban revolutionaries Che Guevara and Fidel Castro, *Playboy* founder Hugh Hefner, astrology researchers Michel Gauquelin and Eugen Jonas, Satanist Anton La Vey, cultist Jim Jones, pop guru Baba Ram Dass, Senator Edward Kennedy, martyred civil rights leader Martin Luther King, Jr., dancer Isadora Duncan and writer Hermann Hesse.

Fidel Castro is a representative case study of the Chiron in Taurus native (see Castro's birth chart, Figure 28). Although labeled a Communist by his critics, Castro's friends in Moscow and Peking scoff at his ideological purity. They know what we Americans have yet to learn, due primarily to the anti-Castro bent of our federal government; namely, that Castro is a nationalist who follows no party line. Whatever lip service he may pay to Marx or Lenin, Castro's

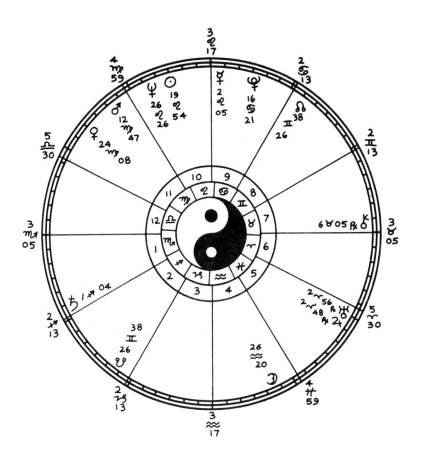

Figure 28. Natal horoscope (Tropical/Placidus) of Fidel Castro, born
11:00 EST (16:00 UT), August 13, 1927, at Biran Cuba
(20N45, 75W30). Data source: Marc Penfield, *2001: The
Penfield Collection.* Seattle, WA: Vulcan Books, 1979.

real mentor has always been Jose Marti, the George Washington of Cuba. He once boasted that, as a student at Havana University, he ready very little of Marx and Lenin but a great deal of Jose Marti. Whereas Marti's career ended in a Spanish ambush on May 19, 1895, Castro has so far been a good deal more fortunate than his mentor. He has made Marti's dream of an independent Cuba, free of Yankee imperialism, a reality. In the process he has alienated the United States, but that's par for the course in any Latin American nationalistic movement.

Castro's is a Full Moon birth chart, the Sun in Leo in the tenth house loosely opposed by the fourth house Aquarian Moon. Chiron sits on the Descendant, in T-Square configuration to the Ascendant and Midheaven. Jupiter and Uranus, both retrograde, are conjunct in Aries, an auspicious conjunction for a revolutionary if ever there was one. In 1953, when Castro first tried to overthrow the Batista government, his progressed Moon had moved to a square aspect with natal Chiron. The coup failed, and Castro went to prison. Upon his release in 1955, he set about planning another revolution, just as Chiron in the heavens squared his natal Chiron. On January 1, 1959, as transiting Chiron opposed Castro's natal Sun, Batista fled — Cuba was Castro's.

CHIRON IN GEMINI

Awareness is the keynote for persons born under this Chiron sign, whose prime existential mission is to understand the way we think in order to effect changes in our mental realities. With an instinctive intuition into the workings of human consciousness, these people seem to have a direct link to the mass mind. Often they are masters of the various media through which people communicate, and they can use this mastery to manipulate the way we think about ourselves and the world. Their principal lessons in life often center around problems that can only be solved through new ways of perceiving and thinking about the world around us. Their mentors appear as persons who offer new perspectives, new constellations of awareness.

Natives of Chiron in Gemini may find that the Quest for selfhood leads them into teaching roles of one kind or another. However they are not teachers in the sense of people who merely transmit information. Rather they are teachers or role models of new perspectives, because they believe that the solution to any problem begins with changing the way people think about it. Crusaders under many banners, those born under this Chiron sign have multiple interests and many irons in the fire at any given time.

Examples of this natal Chiron sign include quixotic California governor Jerry Brown, politically active and controversial actresses Jane Fonda and Vanessa Redgrave, TV personality/author Dick Cavett, pop guru Werner Erhard, feminist writer Gloria Steinem, Spanish King Juan Carlos, and singers Elvis Presley and Merle Haggard.

Jane Fonda is an obvious exemplar of Chiron in Gemini (for her natal horoscope, see Figure 29). Chiron plays a part in two major configurations in Fonda's birth chart, a T-Square to the fifth house Sun in Sagittarius and eighth house Saturn in Pisces, and a yod (the Y-shaped pattern variously known as the Finger of God, Hand of Fate, Finger of Fate, etc.) to the first house Moon in Leo and the sixth house Jupiter in Aquarius. It's a complex chart, with several distinctive celestial patterns, some tighter (i.e. more exactly aspected) than others.

Fonda's advocacy of controversial causes has won her many admirers and not a few critics. I recall some of my Vietnam veteran friends lamenting their inability to shoot her plane down when she visited Hanoi. And it would come as no surprise to learn that she might be on the nuclear industry's hit list. Fonda first appeared on screen at age eighteen, as Chiron transited her natal Jupiter and Descendant. In the late 1960's, as Chiron transited her natal Saturn and entered the ninth house, she became active in the anti-war movement. Her first Academy Award (for "Klute") came in 1972, as Chiron in the heavens trined Fonda's natal Ascendant. A second Oscar came in 1979 (for "Coming Home"), as Chiron transited her natal Midheaven. Along the way she joined forces with radical Tom Hayden (in 1973, coincident with Chiron's transiting trine to her natal Venus), and gave her all on behalf of Hayden's ill-starred 1976 senatorial campaign.

CHIRON IN CANCER

Tradition and emotions are key learning experiences for those born under this Chiron sign. Attuned to the past and deeply sensitive, the native of Chiron in Cancer may be a folk hero or an infamous legend. (It is possible to be one or both and still be known only within one's private circle of acquaintances and friends — it's the archetype that counts, not the publicity.) Whether applauded or condemned by the judgement of time or their peers, these people believe deeply in whatever they do. Their actions, however controversial, stem from a deep conviction that what they are doing will somehow make this a better world, right a wrong of long-standing, or prepare the way for some brighter day. Mentors for these people

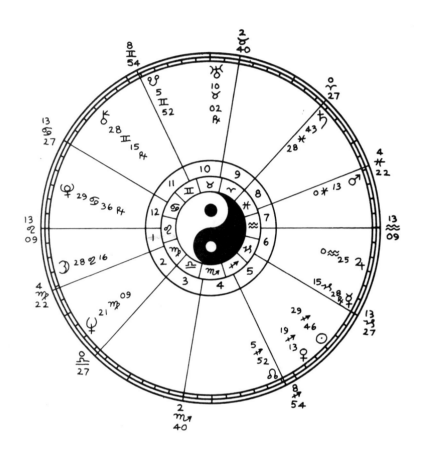

Figure 29. Natal horoscope (Tropical/Placidus) of Jane Fonda born 19:57 EST (00:57 December 22 UT), December 21, 1937, at New York, New York (40N45, 73W57). Data source; LMR, POW.

tend to be folklore idols, whose example inspires the native to preserve and promote some cultural ideal.

There is an element of populism in these people, a certain appreciation for values which have their origin in the masses. They are proud of their roots, and yearn to make others appreciate traditional cultural legacies. Whether their lives are public or private, these people leave their mark. They may seem anachronistic, as if cast up from another time (usually the past), but they are very much in the here and now. For them, the Quest is an emotionally charged revitalization of the past, and it always leads to the creation of a reality that will long be remembered.

Examples of those born under Chiron in Cancer include singer/songwriter Bob Dylan, politically active singers Joan Baez and Anita Bryant, feminist writer Germaine Greer, mystic alchemist Allesandro di Cagliostro, astrologer/writer Marc Edmund Jones, Beatle Ringo Starr, political activist (and former pupil of the youthful Guru Mahara Ji) Rennie Davis, and assassin Lee Harvey Oswald.

The natal horoscope of Bob Dylan (see Figure 7) well illustrates the meaning of Chiron in Cancer. Conjunct the eighth house cusp in this chart, Chiron lies at the midpoint between the Neptune-North Node conjunction in Virgo in the sixth house and the four-Planet Taurus stellium in the ninth (Moon, Jupiter, Saturn and Uranus). As the only Cancer Planet in Dylan's chart, Chiron holds the key to an essential feature of his career as a musical artist; namely his identification with various populist traditions. Although often characterized as leading the vanguard of American music in some respects, Dylan has in fact always been rooted in one traditional role or another, beginning first with his Woody Gutherie folk music, then his street people/working class period, and then most recently his espousal of Fundamentalist Christianity. In each case the artist embraced and gave form to a populist movement.

Dylan's emergence and development as a popular musical artist significantly coincides with major Chiron aspects in relation to his birth chart. The period of emergence, roughly 1960-62, parallels Chiron's transit of the first decanate (i.e. the first ten degrees) of Pisces — this transit saw a conjunction to his natal Mars, a square aspect to his natal Sun and then in mid-1963 a square to natal Venus. All these configurations point to a tremendous drive toward self-fulfillment. A major turning point came in July of 1966 with Dylan's nearly fatal motorcycle accident, a brush with death that seems to have forced him to take stock of himself in radical fashion. It coincided with transiting Chiron's simultaneous opposition to natal Neptune and the Moon's North Node and square to Dylan's Ruling

Planet, Mercury; also a moderately close square to the Ascendant, the window of self-projection in any horoscope. Having drawn from a number of populist cultural movements over the years (e.g. civil rights, psychedelics and zen), Dylan turned around 1980 to Fundamentalist Christianity, just as his progressed Chiron formed the classic yod ("Finger of God") pattern to natal Moon-Saturn conjunction and the Ascendant. A new direction is possible in the period from 1982 to early 1984, as the progressed aspect breaks up coincident with transiting Chiron's passage through the natal Taurus stellium and on to the natal Sun.

CHIRON IN LEO

The legendary nobility of this Sign puts Chiron in a most distinctive light. Those born under Chiron in Leo stand out (or try to) from the crowd in one way or another. Their innate sense of style and grandeur can become for them the very crucible of life. To inspire, to awe and to create pleasure are key focal points for these people. For them, life is to be enjoyed, savored as the ultimate act of creation. Important learning experiences for these Chiron natives tend to center around pride and pleasure. Their primary mentors are dramatic figures who inspire, men and women whose charismatic presence seems to set them apart from ordinary mortals.

Recognition and esteem mean a lot to these people, for whom the greatest failing in life would be to go unnoticed. If they can't earn your admiration, they will be satisfied if they can at least get your attention. Whether as public or private figures, human existence is for them a stage and they are the stars. For them the Quest for self-fulfillment is a worthy enough goal in itself, but it can mean ever so much more if it can be an inspiration (positive or negative) to others. In their individuation process, the pursuit of excellence is in itself a tremendously valuable learning experience, no matter what the ultimate result. Sometimes their greatest lessons come at the very pinnacle of success, which may prove to be the precipice of disaster. Until they learn that "pride goeth before a fall," those born under Chiron in Leo can face many a rough tumble. Yet even if they do fall they are remembered, and in that the Chiron in Leo native takes great satisfaction.

Examples of those born with Chiron in Leo include "Happy Hooker" Xaviera Hollander, civil rights activist Jesse Jackson, ill-starred rock idols Jimi Hendrix and Janis Joplin, singer and film star Barbra Streisand, fantasy writer/philologist J.R.R. Tolkien, chess grandmaster Bobby Fischer, heavyweight boxing champion Muhammad Ali, and all the Beatles except Ringo Starr.

John Lennon is just about as much a paragon of the Chiron in Leo native as anyone could be. Conjunct Pluto in the fifth house of his horoscope, the Centaur Planet is also in opposition to the Aquarius Moon, sextile the Libra Mars and semisextile the Virgo Venus. Lennon's Quest was obviously very much involved with the Beatles and that musical group's phenomenal public success. The element of public acceptance ties in nicely with Chiron's close (three degrees) aspect to the eleventh house Aquarius Moon, as the Moon is traditionally regarded as signifying the public and the eleventh house relates to one's hopes and wishes. Venus and Mars (especially as the latter is in the artistic sign Libra) emphasize the musical direction of Lennons' drive for self-fulfillment, and the fifth house Chiron itself points to one whose Quest is patterned around creativity and young people — such as the young people who were (initially, at least) the Beatles' audience.

Lennon's musical Quest was, to borrow a title from the Beatle songbook, a long and winding road. It began in 1956, when Lennon and McCartney met, coincident with Lennon's progressed Sun-Chiron square and Mercury-Uranus opposition. The following year Lennon and McCartney formed their first band, the "Nurk Twins", just as Lennon's progressed Moon squared his natal Jupiter-Saturn conjunction. McCartney brought George Harrison into the group in 1958, when they became known as "The Quarrymen", simultaneous with Lennon's progressed Moon conjoining natal Venus and progressed Mars quincunx to the natal Jupiter-Saturn conjunction. The progressed Mars aspect to Saturn is ironically significant in view of the group's new name — traditionally, Saturn is said to rule mines and quarries. In 1959 the group initiated a number of name changes as Chiron in the heavens sextiled Lennon's natal Ascendant and trined his Descendant (the latter being of course the cusp of the House of Partners) — they were variously known as "Johnny and the Moondogs", the "Silver Beatles" and ultimately "The Beatles".

The Beatles came into their own as a pop music phenomenon in 1962, when drummer Pete Best was replaced by Ringo Starr. Although announced on August 1, the decision was apparently made simultaneous with the solar eclipse of July 31. This eclipse fell in Lennon's fifth house, less than three degrees from the Chiron-Pluto conjunction. At the time, transiting Chiron trined Lennon's natal seventh house Mercury. The group began breaking up in 1966 by Lennon's account, coincident with his meeting Yoko Ono — under the auspices of transiting Chiron's opposition to natal Neptune. The Beatles' last public performance and Lennon's marriage to Ono took place in 1969, as transiting Chiron trined Lennon's natal Chiron and opposed his natal Mars. The transiting Chiron-trine-Chiron is especially significant in view of Lennon's later statement that Yoko Ono was his mentor, his teacher. As indicated earlier, Chiron signifies one's mentor, as well as one's Quest. Lennon's Chiron strongly aspects his Aquarian Moon, which signifies the woman in his life, and his mentor Yoko Ono was born with the Sun in this sign.

Lennon's Quest came to an end (in this life, at any rate) on December 8, 1980, the day after a New Moon (in his Eighth House) that formed part of a yod configuration to his natal Jupiter-Saturn conjunction and Sun. At the time of the assassination, Pluto had come to the Descendant of Lennon's natal chart, Jupiter and Saturn were conjunct in the heavens (as they had been when he was born), and transiting Chiron had come to the degree of his natal Jupiter-Saturn conjunction.

It's interesting to speculate on the nature of John Lennon's personal Quest for self-transformation. Certainly the Beatle experience was a part of his Quest, and that alone serves to indicate how some people's Quest can become public property. But clearly Lennon's Quest had an intimate, personal side the public may never have glimpsed — and that's the part we can only speculate about. From Lennon's own account of it, his children seem to have been an important element of his own transmutation — which is appropriate in view of Chiron's position in the fifth house, the house of Children among other things.

CHIRON IN VIRGO

Tremendous critical attention to practical details is a hallmark of those born under the Virgo Chiron, whose motto may as well be, "Waste not, want not." Shrewd observers of human behavior and the world at large, they quickly size up the situation in which they find themselves, learn the rules of the game, and then play to win. Dedicated to the pursuit of success (if not excellence), these people are adept at affecting behavior patterns that will help them to accomplish their objectives. In short, they will do whatever it takes to get them what they want, no matter how outrageous their actions may seem to others.

Key learning experiences for natives of Chiron in Virgo tend to focus on issues like self-control and discrimination. Whether it is possible to choose good from bad or anything else from its polar opposite is a crucial concern for these people. In an uncertain world where human understanding is always only relative at best, those born under this Chiron sign pursue absolute truth, even if the means they employ are at times questionable. Mentors appear to these people as persons who are productive and in control of themselves, who seem to know what they want and how to get it. One of the greatest lessons they must face is that control and certainty are at best illusions, at worst outright deceptions. Having mastered this lesson in one form or another, the Chiron in Virgo native can become as a magician, a creator of illusions which have the appearance of reality.

Examples of those born under Chiron in Virgo include Marxist radical Angela Davis, Nazi leader and occultist Rudolf Hess, novelist and psychedelic pioneer Aldous Huxley, Soviet Premier Nikita Krushchev, singers John Denver, Peter Townshend and Mick Jagger, actress Jacqueline Besset and actors Walter Brennan and Jimmy Durante; gurus Meher Baba and Paramahansa Yogananda, philosopher Friedrich Nietzsche and tennis champ Billie Jean King.

Paramahansa Yogananda is an especially fascinating example of the natal Chiron in Virgo (see Yogananda's birth chart Figure 30). Chiron in this horoscope is rising, less than five degrees from an exact conjunction with the Ascendant, the window of selfhood. The Centaur Planet is trine the Moon's North Node, square the Neptune-Pluto conjunction and quincunx Mars. These are powerful and at the same time challenging aspects, quite appropriate for one whose own Quest gave rise to the organization known as the Self-Realization Fellowship. Himself the beneficiary of a guru-chela relationship, Yogananda became a guru to many thousands of people around the world.

Based on his own account of it, Yogananda was called to his Quest before birth. As an infant his mother carried him in her arms to a mass audience with her own guru, Lahiri Mahasaya. Mahasaya took notice of mother and child, beckoned them to him, and pronounced then and there that the boy would be a great yogi who would "carry many souls to God's kingdom." A significant turning point in Yogananda's life came around age twelve, some fourteen months after his mother's death, when he received a psychically materialized amulet that "came from teachers of past lives." A progressed Venus-Chiron trine was in effect at the time. At age fourteen he met his guru, Sri Yukteswar, as Chiron in the heavens trined Yogananda's natal Saturn.

After years of spiritual development Yogananda left India for the United States in August, 1920, under the aegis of transiting Chiron's opposition to natal Saturn. His arrival in October of that year coincided with the onset of a progressed Moon-Chiron conjunction. While in America Yogananda established the Self-Realization

95

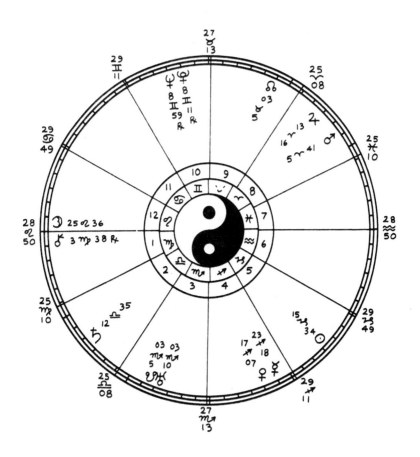

Figure 30. Natal horoscope (Tropical/Placidus) of Paramahansa
Yogananda, born 20:38 LMT (15:04:04 UT), January 5,
1893, at Gorakhpur, India (25N35, 83E29). Data source:
LMR, ABC.

96

Fellowship organization, as a means of helping others in the Quest. His death on March 7, 1952, which he would have said was only a transition, coincided with progressed Venus' opposition to natal Chiron and transiting Sun's conjunction with the progressed Sun. Venus' involvement points to a peaceful transition, and indeed it was — by all accounts Yogananda was fully conscious and very much at peace at the moment of his *mahasamadhi* (a yogi's final conscious exit from the body).

CHIRON IN LIBRA

The Centaur Planet in the seventh sign portends a focus on relationship, both concretely and in the abstract. Personal relationships are important to these people, who seek self-understanding in the ethereal interface between one self and another. To understand oneself, for the native of Chiron in Libra, is to comprehend one's impact on others. The strictly personal realm aside, harmony in general fascinates these people. To make disparate elements work together with one purpose constitutes ultimate existential fulfillment for those born under this Chiron sign.

Their mentors appear as artists, whose all-encompassing vision creates an aesthetic order from the mysterious matrix of chaos. When at last they master one level or another in their personal Quest, the Chiron in Libra natives learn that harmony is a rapture that dwells within or through the perceiver, not a technique belonging exclusively to the artist. To evoke this rapture in others is the ultimate Quest for these people, who measure their own personal meaning in terms of the appreciation for harmony and order they create in those around them.

Along with Virgo, Libra is one of the rarest Chiron signs, because the Centaur Planet spends so little of each orbit in this sector of the zodiac. It seems a strangely significant irony that the Chiron sign which symbolizes one whose self-fulfillment lies in the area of creating shared harmony is, by a process of natural selection, the most uncommon type of human being: Such is the singular destiny of those born with Chiron in Libra.

Examples of the Chiron in Libra native include feminist/theosophist Annie Besant, singers Linda Ronstadt, Bette Midler and Dolly Parton, pop/rock musicians Eric Clapton and Stephen Stills, FBI Director J. Edgar Hoover, conductor Arthur Fiedler and entertainers George Burns and Buster Keaton.

My favorite example of Chiron in Libra is Annie Besant. I suppose one could cite J. Edgar Hoover as an example of the law and

97

order meaning of Libra, or any of the above mentioned entertainers as characteristic of the aesthetic nature of the seventh sign. However, I believe that Annie Besant is by far the most intriguing representative of Chiron in Libra, perhaps because she is not as well known as the others, generally speaking, even though she deserves much more recognition than is commonly accorded her. Located in the seventh house of Besant's natal horoscope, Chiron makes two quite potent aspects — a trine to Neptune and an opposition to Pluto (see Besant's birth chart, Figure 20).

The opposition Chiron forms to Pluto is symbolic of Besant's involvement with feminism in general and birth control in particular. Pluto is traditionally associated with, among other things, sex, death and regeneration. In 1877, the year Besant was arrested and tried on a morals charge stemming from her promotion of birth control information, Chiron in the heavens passed right over the degree of Pluto in Besant's natal chart. The publicity given to Besant's trial served as an inspiration to the American feminist, Margaret Sanger, who many years later helped raise the money to bankroll the research which eventually led to the development of birth control pills.

Besant's natal Chiron-Neptune trine symbolizes her association with the Theosophical Society. Neptune traditionally signifies mysticism, and the Theosophical Society is nothing if not mystical. In 1907, the year she assumed the Presidency of the Theosophical Society in India, Chiron in the heavens was in Aquarius — the Sign of Besant's natal Neptune. Besant held that office until her death in 1933, which was the year transiting Chiron formed a stressful square aspect to Besant's natal Neptune.

CHIRON IN SCORPIO

Self-transformation is a central issue for persons born under this Chiron sign, whose lives are a continual process of metamorphosis. Sex, death and regeneration are common elements of the human experience which are astrologically represented by the eighth sign. Chiron's presence here means that one's life is radically transformed through these and related experiences. For instance an intimate acquaintance with death can play an important role in the life of someone born with Chiron in Scorpio, for whom a close encounter with the Grim Reaper leaves an indelible impression. For the native of Chiron in Scorpio, a mentor may manifest as someone who seems to have conquered death; or conversely as someone who has been utterly overthrown into the abyss of nonbeing. In either case the mentor's example revitalizes the individual, whose life may thereby become a moment for the best (or worse) potentials of the vital force in all of us. Alternatively, the Chiron in Scorpio native may, through his or her own personal experience with death, become a mentor to others.

As it is with death, so it is with all other symbolic dimensions of the eighth sign. Whether it be death, sex, regeneration, control, domination or the mysteries of occultism, those born under Chiron in Scorpio will find that their Quest in life will center around some Scorpionic concern. Regeneration is the keyword here. Some people find it in sex, others in wealth (which is a mundane form of control), still others in the powers of magick (and by that I do not mean mere sleight-of-hand). In any case the individual discovers some area of experience which is in some way taboo, and which yields up a feeling of great vitality and power. Through such a pursuit, the native of the Scorpio Chiron finds an essential key to his or her destiny.

Examples of persons born under this Chiron sign include a number of rather bizarre rock musicians, such as Alice Cooper, Elton John and David Bowie, as well as a few other public figures for whom the shadow of death has a very real meaning — people like Arlo Guthrie, Bernadette Devlin, Gregg Allman and star-crossed pilot Amelia Earhart. Additional examples would have to include controversial Israeli psychic superstar Uri Geller, U.S. Senator Magaret Chase Smith, singers James Taylor, Leo Sayer and Tommy James, actresses Farrah Fawcett-Majors and Kim Darby, and Israeli Prime Minister Golda Meir.

Uri Geller is a prime example of Chiron in Scorpio (see Geller's birth chart, Figure 9). By his own admission, his chief concerns are wealth, power (the psychokinetic variety) and the opposite sex — not necessarily in that order. And he too experienced a close brush with death, when he was wounded by machinegun fire in the Arab-Israeli war of 1967. Geller claims that his psychic powers were first made manifest coincident with a mystical UFO experience he had as a child on Christmas Day, 1949. At that very moment, Chiron in the heavens opposed Geller's natal Uranus and North Node, signifying an electrifying encounter with higher powers. Indeed, Geller was knocked unconscious during the experience. From that moment on, Geller claims, he was blessed with clairvoyance and telepathy. Three-and-a-half years later, Geller's unique abilities were expanded to include psychokinesis, the ability to manipulate matter by mental power alone, without the use of any physical contact. Geller's discovery of his psychokinetic talents came at a time when Chiron in the heavens formed a yod (Finger of God) configuration to his natal Moon-Venus-Jupiter conjunction in Scorpio and Uranus in Gemini.

CHIRON IN SAGITTARIUS

As the celestial representative of the Centaur Chief, Sagittarius is the sign of the seeker, the teacher, the adventurer. Those born during Chiron's stay in the ninth sign partake of all these roles. Curious, daring and possessed of boundless optimism, they are eager to explore the frontiers of experience to the limits of their ability. They seek in some way to uplift others by their example, to inspire everyone to realize their potential to the utmost. In their eyes the greatest mentor is noted not merely for achievement, but for setting others on the path toward greatness.

For those born with Chiron in Sagittarius, life is a great adventure, a long trek toward ultimate enlightenment. With each new experience along the way they seek new revelations, to be remembered and transmitted for the benefit of those who may follow. More inclined to be generalists than specialists (a jack of all trades rather than a master of one), they find fulfillment in multiplicity. Although they may be deep thinkers, those born under this Chiron sign cannot be confined to an ivory tower existence. Their aim is to experience life to the fullest (regardless of the risks), never merely to meditate on its meaning. Like Hesse's Siddhartha, when offered enlightenment secondhand from a spiritual master, they invariably prefer to win it firsthand no matter what the cost.

Examples of the Chiron in Sagittarius native include Olympic decathlon medalist Bruce Jenner, Princess Anne of England, jazz great Louis Armstrong, film director Alfred Hitchcock, actors Humphrey Bogart and James Cagney, actresses Lucie Arnaz and Cheryl Ladd, novelist Ernest Hemingway and Mormon leader Brigham Young.

Ernest Hemingway serves as well as anyone to illustrate the Chiron in Sagittarius archetype (see Hemingway's chart, Figure 31). Of all the Planets in his natal horoscope, Chiron makes the closest aspect to the Ascendant (the point of self-projection), being less than half a degree from an exact square to that point. Hemingway's lifestyle was quintessentially Sagittarian as befits his Chiron sign. Besides being one of the great writers of his time (winner of the Nobel and Pulitzer Prizes), he was also a big game hunter, a deep sea fisherman and an inveterate world traveler. Add to this the fact that his whole life was one great revelry (a moveable feast interrupted only by occasional periods of well-earned convalescence), and it

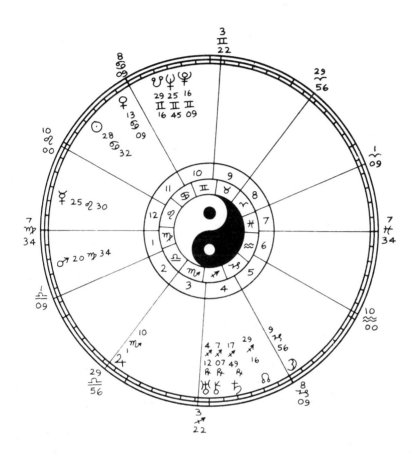

Figure 31. Natal horoscope (Tropical/Placidus) of Ernest Hemingway, born 0:800 CST (14:00 UT), July 21, 1899, at Oak Park, Illinois (41N53, 87W47). Data source: LMR, ABC.

is unmistakably clear that Hemingway's personal Quest is nothing if not a monumental tribute to the meaning of the ninth sign.

Hemingway's life was so full of highlights that it is hard to select only a few to illustrate significant turning points. In 1918, as transiting Chiron trined his natal Sun, Hemingway became an ambulance driver for the Red Cross on the Italian front. (He had tried to get into World War I as a soldier, but was rejected because of his defective eyesight.) In July of that year, just as his progressed Chiron went direct in motion, Hemingway was severely wounded by mortarfire. When the war was over and he had recovered, Hemingway returned to the U.S. and then got a job with the Toronto *Star*. Under the aegis of a trine from transiting Chiron to his natal Chiron, Hemingway left for Paris in 1921. From then on, excepting only a few brief stays in the United States, he was a citizen of the world.

The Sun Also Rises, one of Hemingway's many great books and the first to attract widespread public notice, was published in 1926, simultaneous with transiting Chiron's opposition to the author's natal Jupiter. During the Spanish Civil War, as Chiron transited across his natal Neptune and on to natal Venus, Hemingway fought on the side of the Loyalists, later writing about his experiences in *For Whom The Bell Tolls*. As a war correspondent in Europe in 1944, he ran afoul of the Geneva Convention for joining up with resistance forces to fight the Germans. With transiting Chiron then conjunct his natal Mars, where else could his Quest have taken him?

A lesser man might have counted winning the Nobel Prize (as Hemingway did in 1954, for *The Old Man And The Sea*) the highlight of his life. Transiting Chiron then opposed his natal Sun and formed a Finger of God configuration to natal Mercury and Neptune. Yet it was not a happy time for Hemingway, due in part to slow-healing injuries which resulted from a pair of plane crashes in Africa earlier in the year, and also because the publicity attached to the Nobel Prize was a severe drain on his personal energies. Certainly the worst came for him on July 2, 1961, the day Hemingway took his own life, at a time when Chiron in the heavens was crossing over the degree of his natal Descendant.

CHIRON IN CAPRICORN

This Chiron position signifies a survivor, one whose aim is to prevail (and if possible, prosper) despite any adversity. Power and status are important to these people, who measure their own self esteem through the eyes of others. If they seem traditional or conservative in any way it is because of their desire to conquer time, to preserve some element of their lives despite the transience of the human condition. If they seem radically revolutionary, it is because they fear losing their own identity in the morass of the status quo. If they seem ruthless or desperate, it is because they know full well how brutal and tragic life can be.

Somber of thought and disposition, natives of Chiron in Capricorn are like the man who was chased by a tiger until he lost his footing and fell off a cliff. Tumbling over the precipice, the man managed to catch hold of a wild and wickedly thorned berry bush growing out of the face of the cliff. His hold was precarious at best and owing to the thorns very painful, and he knew it would be only a matter of minutes before he would lose his grip and fall to his death on the rocks below. And yet in those last few moments the man plucked a berry from out of the thorns, ate it, and decided it was the sweetest fruit he had ever tasted. So it is with those born under this Chiron sign, whose tenacity stems from a full awareness that time and chance happen to us all even in this, the best of all possible worlds.

Persons born under this Chiron sign tend to be attracted to mentors who are much older than they are. Often such a mentor is very old indeed — an historical figure from ages past, perhaps, or possibly a previously incarnated identity. Such mentors represent the judgement of eternity, a concept never completely forgotten (not even in deep, dreamless sleep) by the Chiron in Capricorn native.

Examples of the Capricorn Chiron include the tragic modern Sleeping Beauty, Karen Ann Quinlan, heiress and erstwhile revolutionary Patricia Hearst, Japanese emporer Hirohito, "imagineer" Walt Disney, pediatrician Benjamin Spock, anthropologist Margaret Mead, Mormon founder Joseph Smith, writer Anais Nin, singers Janis Ian, Melissa Manchester and Phoebe Snow, and actors Cary Grant and John Houseman.

A poignant illustration of the Capricorn's Chiron's symbolic role as an ultimate survivor is the case of Karen Ann Quinlan (see Quinlan's natal horoscope, Figure 32). Powerfully aspected in this chart, Chiron partakes of a T-Square configuration with Venus in Aries and Neptune in Libra. On April 15, 1975, just as transiting Chiron passed over the degree of her natal Venus, Karen fell victim to an accidental overdose of drugs and liquor (Neptune) at a party (Venus). She went into a coma, and she remains in that state to this day, tragically recalling the myth of the poisoned Centaur who could not die. In March, 1976, the New Jersey Supreme Court ruled that Karen's respirator could be removed, just as Chiron moved to within a degree of an exact square to its natal place in Karen's horo-

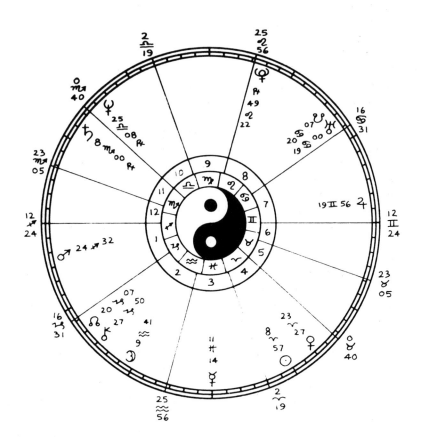

Figure 32. Natal horoscope (Tropical/Placidus) of Karen Ann
Quinlan, born 23:43 EST (04:43 March 30 UT), March 29,
1954, at Scranton, Pennsylvania (41N25, 75W40). Data
source: Doris V. Thompson, *Chart Rectification.* Tempe,
AZ: American Federation of Astrologers, 1978.

scope. The respirator was disconnected on May 17, under the auspices of a transiting Chiron-Saturn square aspect. Contrary to expert medical expectations, Karen continued breathing on her own without any real difficulty. Still surviving, still unconscious, she pursues to this day a personal Quest the likes of which most of us can only surmise.

CHIRON IN AQUARIUS

Past and future are as one for these people, the time travelers of the zodiac. They care not in the least for the emotional depths of water or the commonsense strength of earth, but only for the endless airy vistas of the sky. Eccentric, eclectic and electrifying, the native of Chiron in Aquarius is a human dynamo for whom change is the only constant. Their mentors ask, "Why not?", challenging them to bring dreams into reality. Whether on a personal or social level, these dream images represent the future for those born under this Chiron sign. They fix upon the dream image, and coolly weave it into existence. The ideal becomes the future for them, the future becomes the ideal.

Crackling with a mental energy that can be held in check only by an obvious act of will, these people have a preternatural intensity about them. Their most important learning experiences confront them with the realization that ideals are only the structure of life, not its substance. To know the truth does not insure that one is correct, they must learn, for there are many truths besides one's own. With this awareness those born under the Aquarian Chiron can become advocates of all truths rather than just one, true patrons instead of mere partisans. Failing this a certain fanaticism is likely to manifest in them, leading almost certainly to hubris, alienation and ultimately a Quest ending in tragedy.

Examples of the Aquarian Chiron include actresses Bette Davis, Greta Garbo and Barbara Stanwyck, poet W.H. Auden, organist E. Power Biggs, billionaire recluse Howard Hughes, actor John Wayne and both candidates in the 1964 U.S. presidential election, Barry Goldwater and Lyndon Johnson. (Goldwater is a poetically appropriate name for someone born under Chiron in Aquarius, the Sign of the Water Bearer.) Additional examples are writer Ann Morrow Lindbergh, psychologist Sigmund Freud and existentialist Jean Paul Sartre. The latest crop of this Chiron sign, born from the late 1950s to early 1961, is represented by cultist Maharaj Ji (the "boy guru") and pop singers Andy Gibb, Michael Jackson and Donny and Marie Osmond.

Especially because he presents himself as a Mentor/Guru figure and is accepted as such by his disciples, Maharaj Ji is a symbolically appropriate example of Chiron in Aquarius (see his natal horoscope, Figure 33). This is a powerfully aspected chart, with Sun and Saturn conjunct in Sagittarius at the third house cusp. It is the signature of one who might be the founder of an international religion, especially as the conjunction is in a facile sextile aspect to the Ascendant. Ironically there is a Finger of God aspect in Maharaj Ji's birth chart, from the Sun-Saturn conjunction in Sagittarius to the Libra Ascendant to the cusp of the eighth house. The eighth is of course the house traditionally associated with sex, death, regeneration, inheritance and (last but certainly not least) other people's money. Indeed Maharaj Ji has done rather well in a number of eighth house areas. He has acquired a mansion, a Mercedes-Benz, a wife and children.

The Centaur Planet in Maharaj Ji's horoscope is in the fourth house, part of a Grand Cross in the sensitive angular houses. Chiron opposes a retrograde Uranus in Leo in the tenth house of career, status, ambition and achievement. Both Planets are in square aspect to the Moon's North Nodes, the North Node (the Dragon's Head) being in Scorpio in the first house and the South Node (the Dragon's Tail) in Taurus in the seventh house. A case could be made for interpreting this configuration to mean that the native was a Guru in lives past, and is now experiencing his karma as a need to enlighten and serve others, all the while being tempted by wealth and power.

Maharaj Ji came to the United States from India in 1972, at the age of fourteen. Chiron in the heavens had entered Aries, the sign of new beginnings, and held an opportune sextile angle to Maharaj Ji's natal Chiron. He was received in America as yet another New Age cultist, and his Divine Light Mission won thousands of converts. Followers ecstatically affirmed Maharaj Ji as a Perfect Master, a beatific messiah. What did the Guru have to say for himself? "I'm a groovy kid that's got something you will really like!". Perhaps his optimism stemmed in part from transiting Chiron's providential trine to his natal Uranus. In any case the Perfect Master showed his spiritual stuff by indulging in luxuries — the mansion, the Mercedes, etc.

CHIRON IN PISCES

There is a certain quality about those born under this Chiron Sign which might be called romantic, in the classical sense of that word. Imaginative and more than a little unworldly, these are the fairy tale princesses and knights in shining armor (with a hag or an

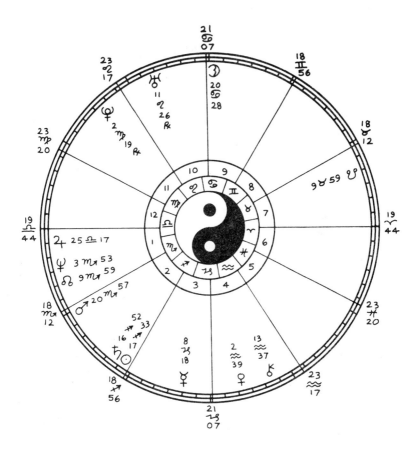

Figure 33. Natal horoscope (Tropical/Placidus) of Maharaj Ji, born 02:30 Zone 5.5 (21:00 UT), December 10, 1957, at Bandrinath, India (30N44, 79E30). Data source: LMR, ABC.

ogre tossed in here and there), the ones who are called upon to perform heroic deeds at great personal risk — or to prevent the accomplishment of such deeds, as the case may be. Life for them can be a mystical crusade in which mundane concerns have no place — a Quest for the Grail, perhaps, or a pursuit of the Ring of Power. Seeing in their mind's eye a better world, they take for granted values that may be totally alien from the perspective of prevailing cultural norms. This personal belief system can create conflict for the Chiron in Pisces native, who may find himself or herself the object of persecution to a greater or lesser extent. In the extreme case this can lead to a variety of martyrdom.

Mentors appear to these people in the guise of individuals who pursue a solitary Quest despite great resistance (even persecution), presevering in spite of everything because their faith does not allow for the possibility of surrender. Whether glorious or tragic in the judgement of their peers, the lives of those born under this Chiron sign take on a certain mythical aura. As archetypes of the hero (or heroine) convinced beyond doubt that his (or her) mission is both necessary and worthwhile, they inspire us to persevere in the pursuit of our own personal Quest, as well as reminding us that belief alone can be a self-contained means of defining one's mission — for better or worse.

Examples of the Piscean Chiron include explorer/adventurers Jacques Cousteau and Thor Hyerdahl, Presidents John Kennedy, Richard Nixon Gerald Ford and Ronald Reagan, evangelists Billy Graham and Oral Roberts, novelist Albert Camus, cultist L. Ron Hubbard, communist patriarchs Karl Marx and Friedrich Engels, inventor-physician-author-parapsychologist Andrija Puharich, astrologer Evangeline Adams, Indian Prime Minister Indira Gandhi and comediennes Lucille Ball and Phyllis Diller.

A peculiarly illuminating representative of the Pisces Chiron is L. Ron Hubbard, the erstwhile science fiction writer who is today better known in his capacity as founder of the controversial Church of Scientology (see Hubbard's natal horoscope, Figure 34). Chiron is part of a Moon-Saturn-Chiron complex in this chart, opposing the Moon in Virgo and sextile the Saturn in Taurus with Saturn, in turn, trining the Moon. Other major configurations in Hubbard's highly complex birth chart include a Grand Trine in Water signs (Mercury in Pisces to Neptune in Cancer to Jupiter in Scorpio) and a T-Square in Mutables (Sun in Pisces squaring the Sagittarius Ascendant as well as Pluto in Gemini at the Descendant).

Hubbard got his start as a writer for pulp magazines in the 1930's, specializing in adventure, travel and science fiction stories.

Figure 34. Natal horoscope (Tropical/Placidus) of L. Ron Hubbard,
born 02:01 CST (08:01 UT), March 13, 1911, at Tilden,
Nebraska (42N03, 97W50). Data source: Doris Chase
Doane, *Progressions in Action.* Tempe, AZ: American
Federation of Astrologers, 1977.

However, by 1935, he had begun researching the basic tenets of what would come to be called *dianetics* — a theory of psychology, Hubbard-style. At the time, transiting Chiron was trining Hubbard's natal Mercury, a fortuitous aspect for psychological endeavors. By his own account, the basic theory of dianetics was fully formed by 1938, under the auspices of an energizing trine from Chiron in the heavens to Chiron in Hubbard's natal horoscope.

The theory of dianetics seems to have lain fallow until Hubbard published an article on the subject early in 1950, coincident with transiting Chiron crossing the author's natal Ascendant and setting off the T-Square to natal Sun and Pluto. With the Planet of the Mentor activating Hubbard's point of self-projection, thousands of seekers responded to the article and hailed him as their guru. A book on dianetics followed the article in short order, and it skyrocketed onto the best seller lists. By 1954 (as transiting Chiron moved to a conjunction with his natal Mars-Uranus conjunction) Hubbard formally incorporated dianetics as the Church of Scientology — the theory had become yet one more religious dogma.

In the years since it was founded, the Church of Scientology has been nothing if not controversial. Critics claim the Scientologists have waged smear campaigns against anyone who has dared to criticize the organization. Meanwhile the governments of Australia, Great Britian and the U.S. have done their best to harass what has become a worldwide cult claiming millions of adherents. By 1974, Hubbard had virtually dropped out of sight, as Chiron transited through his fourth house (the sector traditionally associated with one's roots, one's domicile). He made his home aboard a fleet of boats cruising international waters, far from the controversies stirred up by his brainchild. What's ahead for the Guru of Scientology in the 1980s? Possibly something highly significant along about 1983, when Chiron in the heavens moves to trine both Hubbard's natal Mars-Uranus conjunction and the Centaur's place at the founding of the Church of Scientology. Later that same year the Centaur Planet moves to a strident square aspect of its place in Hubbard's birth chart, insuring that we have not yet heard the last word from the Dianetic Mentor.

CHAPTER 7

SPELUNKING THE CHIRONIAN

Legend tells that Chiron made his home in a cave called the Chironian, a sanctuary the Chief Centaur shared with his half-brother Jupiter near the top of Mt. Pelion. Seekers of wisdom then as now often found it necessary to climb a mountain in order to reach their Guru. But the Chiron myth plainly tells that the sage of sages lives in a cave, clearly an allegory for the unconscious mind. In other words, as any shaman in his or her right mind will tell you, you can climb a mountain in search of illumination if you want, but when that still, small voice finally speaks it will come from within you. The Fool on the Hill climbed there in search of the truth, when all along the object of his Quest was inside him.

Chiron's house in the natal horoscope is the Chironian, the area of life where enlightenment is to be sought and found. According to traditional astrology the houses of a horoscope signify material circumstances of life, areas of experience where the functions represented by the Planets find concrete expression. The Chief Centaur's house position tells where you meet your mentor, as well as where the great existential challenges you face (your Quest, if you will) can be encountered and resolved. Often, like the mythical Centaur's festering wound, these are areas of life that make us uncomfortable, because they seem to represent challenges that are virtually impossible to resolve. But resolve them we must in one way or another, or else face the eternal torment of an unfulfilled destiny.

Seasoned students of astrology may be forgiven for wondering which house system is the right one to use in placing Chiron in the horoscope. After all, which (if any) house system is proper is a question that has never been satisfactorily settled by the astrological community. In all candor I must confess here and now that I have used the Placidus system throughout this book for no other reason than because it is the one used by a majority of astrologers and their

111

students in the United States today. Nevertheless, readers with other preferences are encouraged to follow them. Whichever system works for you will work with Chiron, because in any case it is the practitioner himself or herself that makes the difference — not the system. For that very reason the delineations of Chiron houses that follow, even though they make use of examples calculated in the Placidus system, are equally applicable to any other domification regime.

I am well aware that what I have said here is a paradox, from an empirical point of view. Readers who may be troubled over this seeming paradox are referred to Ptolemy's Cardinal Aphorism, "Judgement must be regulated by thyself, as well as by the science." What I am saying here, Dear Reader, is that the skilled and practiced astrologer may refer to any number of contradictory principles in considering a particular horoscopic judgement. Ultimately it is the faculty of intuition that selects the right rule to follow, the right one to discard.

Red herring domification disputes aside, let's get on with the business of interpreting Chiron's meaning in terms of the houses of the horoscope. In so doing it should be remembered that while Chiron's house position is not in itself sufficient to reveal this Planet's entire personal significance in a particular birth chart, it can be a helpful clue. As always, other factors (such as Chiron's sign and aspects) add important refinements to an understanding of the natal potential. Following are brief delineations of Chiron's house placement, interpreted along the lines of traditional astrology. Intended as symbolic keys only, these interpretations will serve their function only to the extent that you seek to improvise and expand on them, to reformulate them in the light of your own experience. If you regard these delineations as cast in concrete they will only let you down, but if you use them to prime the pump of your own intuition there is no limit to where they might take you.

CHIRON IN THE FIRST HOUSE

Chiron in the first house generally signifies one who personally plays a Chironian role of some kind. He or she may be a teacher, a healer, a mentor or a counselor; someone who acts as a bridge between the In's and Out's, or someone who sets out on an independent course between two extremes in order to dramatize the folly of dogmatic positions in general. Some persons born under this Chiron sector may have a need to see themselves as Great Gurus, while others may devote much of their time and energy to seeking a Guru

112

in someone else. Whether as self-proclaimed Guru or as yeoman Seeker, natives of Chiron in the first house tend to believe that a Spiritual Guide of some sort is just about the most important thing in life. While this orientation predisposes some toward a life of genuine service to others, for some it can lead to extreme ego-tripping (the self-appointed Messiah) or severe ego deflation (the self-deprecating Guru Groupie).

The early years of life generally have an unusually profound influence on First House Chiron natives, setting up patterns of experience for them which carry through in a big way over the long run. Their physical appearance or characteristic manner of self-projection may also put a unique stamp on these people, conferring on them a sense of identity and style that attracts attention wherever they go. Often there is something about these individuals that awakens in others the desire for self-transformation, the motivation to pursue a personal Quest of destiny.

Chiron's presence in the first house is especially emphasized in the lives of persons who come into this world at a time when the Centaur Planet is conjunct the Ascendant (i.e. the cusp of the first house). As a rule, this applies to anyone whose birth chart features Chiron within five degrees of the Ascendant, whether on the twelfth or first house side of that cusp. Examples of Chiron conjunct the Ascendant include singer/comedienne Fanny Brice, Yogi Paramahansa Yogananda, pop guru Werner Erhard (est) and astrologer Evangeline Adams. Others whose natal horoscopes are distinguished by Chiron in the first house (albeit not conjunct the Ascendant) are astrologer Manly Palmer Hall, Japanese Emperor Hirohito, dancer Isadora Duncan, Israel's psychic superstar Uri Geller and his mentor Andrija Puharich, political activist and guru groupie Rennie Davis (a former disciple of Guru Maharaj Ji), the mentor of communism, Karl Marx, nonviolent civil rights martyr Martin Luther King, Jr. and trailblazing scientist Marie Curie.

CHIRON IN THE SECOND HOUSE

Value is an important keyword to this natal Chiron position. Despite its unfortunate commercial connotations, value means far more than just a price tag. The things you value most are the ones you take for granted, the ones which in their absence would have a way of turning your whole life topsy-turvy. With this Chiron placement often comes a strong proselytizing urge, aimed at preserving one's values for posterity by cultivating these values in others. For these natives, fulfillment may consist of developing their various gifts and imparting them as a legacy to others, whose appreciation is accepted as a testimonial to the very value that mean so much to the native. Should they fall prey to the misguided notion that theirs are the only true values, these people can become cynical and manipulative in the extreme. But as long as they realize there can only be dishonor in placing one's own values over and against all others, they are not likely to suffer messianic delusions. The key to self-fulfillment for those born with this Chiron emphasis generally entails learning to handle some natal endowment, perhaps a talent, trait or socio-cultural legacy. Through these and like possessions they are led to a meeting with the mentor who will reveal to them their path of destiny.

Examples of the second house Chiron include chess champion Bobby Fischer, astrologer Ralph Kraum, politician Huey P. Long and violinist Jascha Heifetz (all of whose birth charts feature Chiron conjunct the Second House cusp); as well as sidereal astrologer and historian Cyril Fagan, cultist/writer L. Ron Hubbard, psychologist Carl Jung, medical researcher Jonas Salk, writer/politician Clare Boothe Luce, psychologist Elisabeth Kubler-Ross and tragic coma victim Karen Ann Quinlan.

CHIRON IN THE THIRD HOUSE

Chiron in the third house gives a special emphasis to information processing at many levels. Physical coordination is often highly important to these people, who feel an instinctive need to make mind and body work as one. Some form of technology may play an important role in their lives, because they tend to regard tools as an extension of self. This House placement can be expressed in many different ways, but underlying any particular manifestation is the desire to master a craft and then use that mastery to advance the individual's own self interest: Knowledge is power to the third house Chiron native.

Some of these natives orient their whole lives around a special talent or interest, finding themselves unhappy or ill at ease except when fully engaged in pursuit of the chosen specialization. Others manage to maintain balance, realizing that single-mindedness is a less than truly human state of consciousness. Mastery of some technique or knowledge is in itself an admirable goal, but it is not the end-all and be-all of life for the more developed natives of Chiron in the Third House.

114

Sibling relationships can be a highly significant arena of experience for these people, for whom a brother or sister can represent an important turning point in life. Or the individual may have no siblings at all, giving rise to a sense of loss or isolation. Peer relationships, a sense of fellowship among equals, can be crucial to the pursuit of this native's Quest. When such a person finds his or her mentor, they strike up a relationship characterized more by fraternity (or sorority, as the case may be) than by the more traditional authoritarian bonds commonly thought of in connection with the interaction between mentor and protege.

Chiron is conjunct the third house cusp in the birth charts of tennis champ Chris Evert Lloyd, actor Paul Muni and Happy Hooker Xaviera Hollander. Other examples of Chiron in the third house include astrology publisher Paul Clancy (founder of *American Astrology* magazine), entertainer Gypsy Rose Lee, feminist writer Betty Friedan, Christian Science founder Mary Baker Eddy, skater Sonja Henie, aircraft designer Anthony Fokker, psychoanalyst Sigmund Freud and existentialist Jean Paul Sartre.

CHIRON IN THE FOURTH HOUSE

With Chiron in the fourth house comes a symbolic emphasis on one's roots in life as holding the keys to destiny. Through participation in various social traditions and institutions, the people born under this Chiron placement find personal meaning in terms of a cultural legacy which predates and survives them. God, Motherhood and Apple Pie may be crucial to these Chiron natives, so to speak, because they feel a deep need to partake of something more or less eternal.

While they are personally dedicated to whatever gives them a sense of rootedness and continuity, the Fourth House Chiron natives generally do their level best to extend the sense of identity they feel out into the world at large. It's not enough for them to find their own sense of belonging; they want to spread the word to others, to share what they consider a more or less common birthright. At the same time they are instinctively impatient (to say the least) with anyone who is intolerant of (or disrespectful toward) the values they hold in high regard.

The family unit, whether nuclear or extended (and usually the latter) plays a prominent role in the lives of these people, who have a strong sense of familial ideals and standards. As adults, whether they have children or not, they may assume some kind of parental role. Whether by attempting to live up to a standard of conduct

115

which they hope will be an inspiration to others, or by actually attempting in some way to nurture others as a parent would a child, people born with Chiron in the fourth house can exert a powerful influence on their social environment.

A prime example of the fourth house Chiron in many respects is writer Ernest Hemingway (Papa to his friends), who was born with the Centaur Planet conjunct the IC, or fourth house cusp. Anyone whose natal horoscope features Chiron within five degrees of the IC (either on the third house side or the fourth house side of that point) will generally exhibit strong characteristics of Chiron in the fourth house. Additional examples of the fourth house Chiron include animator/imagineer Walt Disney, astronaut/politician John Glenn, comedienne Judy Canova, actors Jackie Cooper and Mickey Rooney, actresses Helen Hayes and Tallulah Bankhead, writers Anais Nin, Hermann Hesse and Kurt Vonnegut, singer Joan Baez, psychedelic guru/exopsychologist Timothy Leary, baseball legend Babe Ruth, politician Edward Kennedy, Mormon leader Brigham Young and communist guru/revolutionary Nicolai Lenin.

CHIRON IN THE FIFTH HOUSE

Pomp and circumstance mean practically everything to those born under this Chiron placement. Whether through natal endowment or careful study (or both, as is usually the case), they tend to have a knack for understanding and manipulating human psychology. This talent can be used to direct others to do the native's bidding; or it may be used for its own sake, for the pure joy of creation, as an artist uses color and form or as a musician uses sound and time. In any event the native finds personal fulfillment in being able to stir the hearts of those with whom he or she comes in contact.

Their mentors and essential Quests are to be found through some role they play or project. In many cases these people grow into a role they began playing while still children. As children will, they discover themselves in the roles they take on; as actors so often do, the play becomes so real to them that they find it hard to remember what is real and what is role. Children remain important in the lives of Fifth House Chiron natives even when they reach adulthood: Their own or someone else's children profoundly affect these Chiron natives, irrevocably altering their course in life.

Regardless of whatever moral judgement their peers may bestow on them, these people make their mark through a personal Quest aimed at stirring the hearts and igniting the imaginations of their fellow human beings. They decide early in life (generally no later than adolescence) that they are in some sense special, and from that moment on they aim to make others realize it too.

Chiron is conjunct the fifth house cusp in the natal horoscopes of Nazi propaganda minister Joseph Goebbels and U.S. politician (former presidential candidate) Barry Goldwater. Others whose natal charts feature Chiron in the fifth house (but not conjunct the cusp) are England's Prince Charles, kidnapped heiress-turned-revolutionary Patricia Hearst, author Ann Morrow Lingbergh, witch Sybil Leek, astrologer Sidney Bennett, actresses Dolores Del Rio, Joan Fontaine and Janet Gaynor, actress/ambassador Shirley Temple Balck, singer Barbra Streisand, columnist/TV personality Ed Sullivan, ex-Beatles Ringo Starr and John Lennon, and radical teacher Angela Davis.

CHIRON IN THE SIXTH HOUSE

Discipline is a central issue for those born under this Chiron House. For them, the Quest for self-transformation is seen as a struggle between light and darkness which must be resolved by putting everything — right down to the smallest detail — into a workable and generally rational order. Whatever might not at first fit into this order must be assimilated if possible; and if that is not possible, it must be rationalized, sublimated, suppressed or eliminated.

Health too is a matter of prime concern for these natives. Their health may suffer from an inordinate drive to subject all experiences to a rigid code of order. Or they may have a health problem that requires the development of certain personal discipline. Failure to find a sane and workable balance between mind and matter can hit these people hard: Too much mind over matter, or too little, can lead to a crisis for the native.

Natives of the sixth house Chiron tend to view their vocation as part and parcel of their personal destiny. Their work is their Quest, and vice versa. They want to do good work, or else not to work at all. However they may be judged by their peers, these individuals judge themselves the hardest. Expecting the best of and/or for themselves, they can self-destruct either directly (by their own choice) or indirectly (by forcing others to act) if they fail to live up to their strict standards of performance. When they are happy they are in a blissful state, but when they fall short of what they expect from themselves (or what others expect of them) they can end up paying a high price indeed. What is the course of wisdom in this situation? Perhaps it would be to aim a little short of absolute, consistent adherence to principle — but that is not an easy compromise for the sixth house Chiron to make.

Chiron occupies the sixth house cusp in the natal horoscopes of nonviolent political guru Mahatma Gandhi, ex-Beatle Paul McCartney, actress Jean Harlow and humanitarian physician Tom Dooley. Others whose birth charts feature Chiron in the sixth house include U.S. Presidents John Kennedy, Richard Nixon and Jimmy Carter, singer/actress Liza Minnelli, actor Jackie Coogan, columnist Walter Winchell, gangster Legs Diamond, aviator James Doolittle, astrologer Grant Lewi and Egyptian King Farouk I.

CHIRON IN THE SEVENTH HOUSE

Justice, equity and equality are much on the mind of the seventh house Chiron native. For this one, the pursuit of destiny lies in the area of relationships, whether these be relationships between two or more persons or more abstract relationships such as those involving the pursuit of truth, justice and beauty. However they express it, in whatever field, these individuals are deeply concerned with creating a balanced harmony of opposites from out of the chaos of contradictory forces or ideas.

Partnerships of all kinds are crucial to these people, but chief among these are intimate, one-on-one relationships — marriage, living together, even business partnerships can be important focal points of experience. However it may also happen that no one person can fulfill the seventh house Chiron native's need for self-discovery through relationship. In this case the native may seek fulfillment in an impersonal or idealized way, as for example through the bond between the artist and art, or between the artist and the public — perhaps even in the heady psycho-spiritual relationship between God and prophet.

There is little in the way of solitude for the individual born under the seventh house Chiron, whose life is so closely bound up with others. Often this manifests as a life lived largely in the public eye. Self-transformation, for this Seeker, is to be sought outside the narrow limits of the self. This person's Quest leads to other people, any of whom may become a Spiritual Guide under the proper circumstances.

Chiron's seventh house presence is especially emphasized under the aegis of the Centaur Planet's conjunction with the Descendant (cusp of the seventh house). This configuration is effective any time Chiron is within five degrees of the Descendant, whether above it (actually in the seventh house) or below (technically in the sixth house). Examples of those born under the latter category include Mormon patriarch Joseph Smith, People's Temple leader Jim Jones and entertainer Bette Midler. Examples of the seventh house Chiron conjunct the Descendant include writer Upton Sinclair, pilot Amelia Earhart, singer Janis Joplin and physician/theologian/musician Albert Schweitzer. Others born with Chiron in the seventh house (but not conjunct the Descendant) include writer Gloria Steinem, communist Friedrich Engels, social reformer and Theosophist Annie Besant, and musician Bob Dylan.

CHIRON IN THE EIGHTH HOUSE

These persons find the key to their destiny in the experiences traditionally associated with this house, including sex, death, regeneration and hidden things, as well as other people's money and values. In coming to terms with these areas of life, natives of the eighth house Chiron generally undertake some form of heroic Quest leading to radical self-transformation. Some are driven by a deep-rooted anxiety about death to the point that they seek some transcendental meaning underlying the human conditions. Others, disturbed over what they perceive as their condition of social or cultural powerlessness, strive to achieve some kind of control over their fellow human beings — for some this would entail the accumulation of wealth or the pursuit of socio-cultural prestige and authority. Another alternative would be to develop one's psychospiritual power — a factor that motivates many natives of this Chiron house to investigate various forms of occultism.

Regardless of the particular path they take, these natives must eventually face the consequences of their will to power, which is rooted in desire. Mentors often appear to these people in the guise of masters or slaves, persons who either have some control over the native (or someone else) or who are controlled by the native (or someone else) respectively. The revelation afforded by a Spiritual Guide is not always easy to come by, but it can be especially difficult for those born under Chiron in the eighth house. For such as these enlightenment can mean surrender — something they are not accustomed to accepting readily.

Persons whose natal horoscopes feature Chiron in the eighth house include Indian Prime Minister Indira Gandhi (Chiron conjunct the eighth house cusp), gurus Meher Baba and Krishnamurti, artist Yoko Ono, advice columnist Abigail Van Buren, comedian Jack Benny, actress Clara Bow, the Duchess of Windsor, writer Jack Kerouac, tennis champ Billie Jean King, TV journalist Barbara

Walters, astrologer Marc Edmund Jones and transsexual Christine Jorgensen.

CHIRON IN THE NINTH HOUSE

Those born under this Chiron house generally find the path to self-fulfillment a long, long road indeed. If at all intellectually inclined they tend to be deep thinkers, well versed in the subtleties of philosophy and religion. Should they be the anti-intellectual sort, they express the same far-ranging drives in a fashion more concrete than abstract, more on the level of emotion than on the plane of reason. Both types have in common a fundamental urge to be and to experience as much as possible, coupled with a need to assemble all they have thereby gathered into one cohesive whole, whether conceptual or emotional.

Long sojourns in distant lands can figure prominently in their lives. If not, they travel extensively on a more abstract level, through education, creative imagination or some other less than literal means of transport. Their journeys (and often their journals, for they tend to be the type to jot things down) are the means whereby these people stretch their awareness to the breaking point, only to pull everything together with some proof or other creation which they feel is the key to the human condition.

While some of these individuals may be content merely find this key for themselves, most are driven to share their discoveries with as many people as possible. Able to see possibilities that transcend ordinary mundane reality, these people are visionaries with communicable (even highly infectious) dreams. Their long-range impact on their environment is a complex of many factors, but for better or worse they tend to leave a considerable wake behind them.

Examples of the ninth house Chiron come in all varieties, including as tragic a pair as can be found: Adolf Hitler, who borrowed his psychotic Master Race litany in part from philosopher Friedrich Nietzsche; and der Fuhrer's mentor (or one of them at any rate), Nietzsche himself. Additional examples include educator Maria Montessori, actresses Goldie Hawn and Marilyn Monroe, authors Alex Haley and F. Scott Fitzgerald, and astrologers Ernest Grant, Charles A. Jayne, Jr. and Dane Rudhyar. The latter two, you may recall, both predicted the existence of a planet fitting Chiron's description long before the Chief Centaur was discovered by Charles Kowal in 1977. Dane Rudhyar's ninth house Chiron seems especially significant in view of the fact that he has been a longtime sojourner in a land far from his birthplace (born in Paris, Rudhyar has spent most of his life in the U.S.); and also because of his highly philosophical approach to the cosmic art/science.

CHIRON IN THE TENTH HOUSE

Reputation, status, authority and achievement are key focal points for those born under this Chiron house, who always have an eye toward the social dimension of human experience. This focus may be expressed directly in terms of an impulsive pursuit of status, authority, etc.; or it may manifest indirectly as an aversion to these same areas of human experience. In most cases the individual is subject to a combination of both direct and indirect expressions: He or she may reject the very idea of authority, while at the same time striving mightily to become an authority of some sort.

The road to fame and fortune can become a sacred Quest for this individual. It can demand total self-sacrifice and ultimately requires an utter denial of everything but the native's career. Mentors appear to this person as a respected and honored (or at least recognized) over-achiever, someone who serves to inspire the native's ambition, perhaps even personally intervening to open a vocational door here and there. These mentors succeed in their mission to the extent that they help the individual to realize the need to balance one's social and personal energies, or else they fail in the same measure as they cultivate an obsession with reward and status.

Family concerns generally play an important role in molding the tenth house Chiron native's Quest after (or away from) authority. The family structure may be supportive, or so negative as to impel the native to seek or flee recognition in an obsessive way. In either case the individual's orientation to tenth house matters is largely due to his or her experience with the family environment. Parenting in particular is of prime importance: The individual's parents or the individual's role as a parent himself or herself plays a big part in shaping the Quest for self-transformation.

Examples of the tenth house Chiron include ex-Beatle George Harrison, the 18th Century alchemist extraordinaire Allesandro di Cagliostro, occultist Aleister Crowley, singers Judy Garland and Linda Ronstadt, actresses Hedy Lamarr and Ginger Rogers, writers Anne Frank and William Saroyan, labor leader Walter Reuther, politician Hubert Humphrey, aviator Wiley Post, political journalist Jack Anderson, Queen Juliana of the Netherlands, and Ethiopian Emperor Haile Selassie.

121

CHIRON IN THE ELEVENTH HOUSE

As a rule, those born with an eleventh house Chiron have a need to be at the cutting edge of the future. They feel alienated from their environment, and are consequently driven to create a new world in some fashion or another. The status quo invariably strikes them as primitive (at best), and they are not long at a loss when it comes to improving the way things are. Social, political and intellectual matters are usually important to these natives, who take an active interest in these areas of experience. However it would be a mistake to think of the eleventh house Chiron strictly as a signature of intellectualism and/or socio-political involvement: Art, science, ethics, technology, fellowship — all these and other related areas as well are the haunts of those born with the Centaur Planet in this horoscopic sector.

If natives of the eleventh house Chiron seem in some way eccentric (and they usually do), it is in no small measure because they are bound and determined to be different. Generally eclectic, idealistic and intellectual (if not intellectual then a master of some art or craft), this type is no mere offbeat daydreamer. These people are determined in their own fashion to revolutionize some greater or lesser part of the world around them: To remake the world after their own image is an essential part of their Quest.

For these people a mentor is usually someone who blatantly marches to a different drumbeat, someone whose eccentric or otherwise exceptional nature attracts attention and generates controversy. Destiny awaits the native of Chiron in the eleventh house to the extent that he or she attempts to impose ideas and ideals onto the world at large. With the help of a mentor (and sometimes a mentor must be cruel to help), this individual ultimately finds self-transformation through affecting a change in his or her social environment.

Examples of the eleventh house Chiron include atheist activist Madalyn Murray O'Hair and pioneering hypnotist Franz Anton Mesmer (both born with Chiron conjunct the eleventh house cusp); also Theosophical Society co-founder Madame Blavatsky and psychedelic advocate-turned-pop guru Richard Alpert (aka Baba Ram Dass) — both of whom were born with Chiron in the 17th degree of Taurus. (These two horoscopes share a great number of parallels: Both have fire sign Sun, earth sign Mercury, Saturn and Neptune in earth signs, and the same signs on all house cusps — to mention only a few factors.) Additional natives of the eleventh house Chiron are actress/social advocate Jane Fonda, singer/homophobe Anita Bryant, pediatrician Benjamin Spock, politician Edmund G. Brown, Jr., astrologers Rupert Gleadow and Vivian Robson, and actresses Joan Blondell, Celeste Holm and Gene Tierny.

CHIRON IN THE TWELFTH HOUSE

Isolation is always in some sense a keyword for this Chiron type, which symbolizes one who chooses to be as far from the crowd as possible (physically or psychically, as the case may be). Of course no one is an island, so to speak, but to the extent these natives do take part in society they do so by playing a role which is at most merely a fraction of their full individuality. They seem to belong to two worlds (maybe more), and the world of commonsense reality tends not to be their strong suit. Nevertheless some of them play a role that attracts public notice. When this happens the native generally manages to maintain privacy despite the limelight by projecting a deliberate smokescreen. Through misinformation, exaggerated behaviors or otherwise acting out of character, this type is adept at maintaining a private sanctuary even under the most inhospitable circumstances.

Self-imposed solitude is no mere affectation for these people. They are alone with their inner selves not just by choice, but by necessity. Those among them who may be unable to maintain the necessary degree of physical or psychic solitude by their own resources may find such solitude imposed on them by their social environment.

Mentors appear to natives of the twelfth house Chiron as martyrs, persons who sacrifice themselves to atone for the actions of others. In some cases the native may follow the mentor's example to the point of total self-sacrifice. Whatever its mundane outcome, this person's Quest is in some essential respect a solitary path. It is a path of self-transformation, whether personally chosen or imposed by others, that brings the native through a "black night of the soul" — from which no one can emerge who is not transmuted.

Examples of the twelfth house Chiron include anthropologists Margaret Mead and Carlos Castaneda, champion boxer Muhammad Ali, ventriloquist Edgar Bergen, would-be assassin Arthur Bremer and composer George Gershwin; also astrologer Tracy marks, author of a book entitled (appropriately, in this case) *The Twelfth House*.

CHAPTER 8

CHIRON CYCLES

Normally, when one thinks of cycles in an astrological context, one has in mind the time periods the Planets take to return to their natal places or some other significant positions. In this sense, Chiron's orbital period of approximately fifty years is a foremost cycle of the Centaur Planet. At age fifty, give or take a few months, each of us will experience a Chiron return, a conjunction of transiting and natal Chiron. Socially and psychologically speaking, the fiftieth year of life corresponds to something of a peak: It marks the prime, a time when one's labors are most apt to be best rewarded, an interval when one is most likely to have achieved a sense of fulfilled selfhood — if one ever will. In this regard it is symbolically fitting that the Chiron return comes when it does.

At a deeper level, the Chiron return charts a cycle of great spiritual significance. It points out the rhythm of one's personal Quest. This rhythm begins for all practical purposes at birth, an instant at which Chiron's natal position symbolizes one's potential for self-transformation — for the transcendence of what is normally taken for granted as *mere* human nature. The natal potential is constantly operative, to be sure, but it reaches critical peaks of consciousness at intervals corresponding to definite aspects between transiting and natal Chiron. These come, generally speaking, at the quarter and halfway points of the cycle, corresponding to the square and opposition aspects.

The first square comes approximately at age twelve-and-a-half, at a time when one's biopsychic and spiritual consciousness reach a critical point. It is an age of initiation in many cultures and religions, roughly corresponding to a number of important rites of passage, such as the transition from elementary to middle (junior high) school, confirmation and bar (or bat) mitzvah, as well as (in many cases at least) the onset of puberty. Another crucial period is marked by the opposition of transiting Chiron to natal Chiron, approximately at age twenty-five. It is a time when the individual has, as a rule, found an adult niche in terms of career and family life, an epoch when the individual has formed a clear idea of his or her personal Quest, at least in socio-cultural terms. Age thirty-seven-and-a-half roughly speaking, corresponds to the second square from transiting to natal Chiron, a personal epoch that finds the individual looking beyond his or her socio-cultural niche, searching for something more enduring, more significant — more nearly eternal. The first cycle comes to a head with the Chiron return around age fifty, a time when the individual who has found the Quest may experience a plateau of sorts. This is when the prepared and developed Seeker may serve as a mentor to others, if he or she has not already been able to do so. The cycle of course continues as long as one remains in the body — indeed, if one has followed the right Quest, it continues long after the physical life is ended.

It is a matter of curious significance that the Chiron cycle corresponds with the orbital cycle of Sirius B, the invisible (to the naked eye) white dwarf star in orbit around the Dog Star Sirius — the latter being of course the brightest star in the heavens as seen from Planet Earth. In the mystery rites of ancient Egypt, rituals concerned with the Initiate's development as a full-fledged Seeker after the Spiritual Quest, the goddess Isis is presented as a symbol of Sirius and the God Osiris as a symbol of Sirius' Dark Companion — dark in this case meaning *invisible* (just as Sirius B is invisible to the naked eye), according to some who have studied this question closely. In the Eleusinian mystery schools, according to such students as Aleister Crowley and Eliphas Levi, it is said that Osiris is *a black god* — a dark star? Like Sirius B, Chiron is a dark star, in the ancient sense that it is a light in the heavens which cannot be seen by the unaided eye. Also like Sirius B/Osiris, Chiron is a celestial body having a fifty-year period, said to have domain over such human beings as may set out on the Quest for Enlightenment. To the materialist, these coincidences are nothing more than chance correspondence — to the Seeker, they are as a sign in the heavens.

Aside from the cycles of relationship between transiting and natal Chiron, there are a number of other important cycles which are not generally recognized as such. In this case, Dear Reader, I refer to mutual aspects between Chiron and other important focal points in the natal horoscope. Aspects are all too often supposed to be merely static angles, when in fact they are phases in a cycle of relationship. To be born with, say, Mars square Chiron, is to have a natal potential that focuses on a particular phase in the relationship between these two Planets. The relationship itself is a dynamic evolutionary process, symbolically accentuated at intervals corresponding to key phases in the ongoing cosmic cycle which links the two Planets, in this case Mars and Chiron. The Mars-Chiron square, or any other aspect for that matter, makes sense only insofar as it is understood as a significant phase in a rhythmic celestial cycle. The cycle gives meaning to its phases, the phases have no existence apart from the holistic rhythm of which they are a part.

What is said above is a statement of general principles, which take on real form only as they are revealed in particular cases. Therefore we are about to consider various fundamental Chiron cycles and aspects. In so doing, we shall be limited (for the purposes of this discussion, at any rate) to a number of primary cyclic phases (aspects); namely the conjunction, sextile, square, trine, quincunx and opposition. Seasoned students of astrology will immediately notice that this selection of phases is somewhat arbitrary: It leaves out a number of aspect/phases often used by astrologers (such as the quintile, septile, octile, novile, decile, etc.), as well as any number of other harmonic cycles which may be taken as aspect/phases. However it is expected that astrologers whose studies are sufficiently advanced as to require the use of these so-called minor aspects will also be advanced enough to work out for themselves a delineation of these aspect/phases, based on the overall symbolic gestalt of each cycle as a whole. What matters most in each case is the cycle itself, and from that any desired phase may be inferred.

The following discussion is also limited to a selection of fundamental astrological functions in relation to the Centaur Planet. These are the Major Planets, Sol, Luna, Mercury, Venus, Mars, Jupiter, Saturn, Uranus, Neptune and Pluto. This is not to say that other Chiron cycles are unimportant just because they are not specifically treated here. Advanced students of the cosmic art/science may wish to investigate Chiron's relationship with other Minor Planets, the Arabian Parts, hypothetical planets, the Moon's Nodes, etc. And then of course there are the horoscopic angles, the Ascendant, IC, Descendant and MC. Chiron's relationship to these points is implicit in the delineations supplied in the previous chapter. Suffice it to say that there are so many astrological functions, and so many possible aspects, that any selection must be less than complete. Thus in what follows we will encounter a number of fundamental Chiron cycles — not every cycle, to be sure, nor every phase, but a sampling sufficient to serve immediate needs and to suggest directions for further, more comprehensive studies.

SUN-CHIRON

This is approximately an annual cycle in the heavens, which denotes opportunities for the Seeker to determine the nature and direction of the Quest. These opportunities present themselves, often without the Seeker's conscious recognition of the fact, synchronous with Sol's conjunction to Chiron. Critical points in this cycle, which coincide with hard aspects between Sol and Chiron (the square and opposition), symbolize the need for conscious action and decision with regard to the process of self-transformation. The soft aspects (sextile, trine, quincunx) correspond to favorable conditions for pursuing the Quest, provided the Seeker is consciously aware of the need for transmutation — otherwise opportunities may be missed, and the Seeker may not be aware of them until long after the fact.

Natally, the Sun-Chiron cycle refers to the will to power as it relates to self-transformation. Aspects between Sol and the Centaur Planet symbolize distinctive phases in the individual's potential for transforming himself or herself so as to transcend the limitations of mortality. Sun conjunct Chiron (an aspect found in the natal chart of cultist Jim Jones) reveals a strong fusion of will and the Quest. Pride and power await this Seeker, they may even lie in wait for him or for her as in ambush. Sun sextile Chiron (present in the birth charts of Judy Garland, Xaviera Hollander, Maharaj Ji and Gloria Steinem) symbolizes awareness of and possibilities for self-transformation, with an eye toward utilizing one's own Quest as a vehicle for reaching others. Sun square Chiron (a factor in the natal horoscopes of Madame Blavatsky, Amelia Earhart, Werner Erhard, Hubert Humphrey, Marc Edmund Jones, Clare Booth Luce and Yoko One) points to one whose Quest resolves in some sense around the issue of socio-cultural authority. This Seeker may rebel against such authority, and/or may seek to become such an authority. Sun trine Chiron (an aspect found in the birth chart of Indira Gandhi) symbolizes a Seeker whose Quest materializes as creativity and discovery in response to socio-cultural legacies such as tradition, religion and culture. Sun quincunx Chiron (present in the birth chart of Germaine Greer, Janis Joplin and Maria Montessori) suggests one whose Quest is a matter of health, education and welfare — these applying either directly to the Seeker, or indirectly through the Seeker's concern and involvement with health, education and welfare of others. Sun oppose Chiron (found in the birth charts of Aleister Crowley, Jane Fonda and Brigham Young) points to one whose Quest is undertaken in the context of a special relationship with others — typically, he or she is a mentor to others, a guide or Initiator (Psychopomp).

MOON-CHIRON

This is a monthly cycle, roughly speaking. Its cyclic ebb and flow in the heavens signifies the waxing and waning of public awareness of and interest in the Quest, as well as instinctive (largely unconscious) movement toward and away from the possibility of self-transformation. The Moon-Chiron relationship signifies mass currents of feeling with regard to transcending ordinary, mundane human limitations. When Luna conjoins Chiron in the heavens, it is a time of instinctive yearning for the mentor, the alchemist, the one who reveals to humankind the way beyond mortality and matter. At the sextile, trine and quincunx points between these two celestial bodies, conditions favor the release of pent-up energies that can bring the dream of transmutation into concrete existence. At the square and opposition points, instinct and opportunity unite to open channels of awareness and relationship — students find their mentors, mentors find their students, and Quests are undertaken with energy and enthusiasm.

Natally, the Moon-Chiron cycle symbolizes the individual's relationship with what Robert Graves has called The White Goddess — meaning, at the very least, the instinctive, poetic and irrational function in human nature. Aspects between Luna and the Centaur Planet signify critical high points in one's potential for transcending what is commonly perceived as logical, empirical, commonsense reality. They make us conscious of mystery, magick and the eternal dialectic of spirit and matter. The conjunction of Luna and Chiron (present in the birth charts of Paul McCartney and Madame Curie) points to one for whom serendipity is a fact of life — happy accidents, discoveries made seemingly by chance, these are the stock-in-trade of the native. Moon sextile Chiron (found in the natal horoscopes of Jane Fonda, Indira Gandhi, George Harrison, Elisabeth Kubler-Ross and Nicolai Lenin) is a hallmark of the individual with an instinct to capitalize on even the most unlikely opportunity — this one has a knack for being in the right place at the right time, however bizarre the circumstances may seem to someone outside the immediate situation. Luna square Chiron (a natal aspect shared by Muhammad Ali, Allesandro di Cagliostro, Betty Friedan and John Glenn) stands for one who comes on many a tricky crossroads in life — there are sudden changes in fortune, periods of public disfavor or disinterest, difficulties in dealing with the feminine principle whether concretely (as in the case of an individual female) or abstractly (as for instance with reference to femininity, instinct, the psychic force, etc.). Luna trine Chiron (present in the birth charts of Kurt Vonnegut and Linda Ronstadt) is the hallmark of the Restless Seeker, the one whose search for transformation leads to ever new and different settings, yet always seems to revolve around the same issues — issues like fidelity to one's Muse, Spiritual Guide or memory. Moon quincunx Chiron (as represented in the natal charts of astrologer Evangeline Adams, writer Jack Kerouac and educator Maria Montessori) is symbolic of one whose Quest entails service to the masses or to the Muse — to fail in either obligation is perilous in the extreme. And finally, Moon oppose Chiron (present in the birth charts of John Lennon, L. Ron Hubbard, Werner Erhard, Adolf Hitler and Madalyn Murray O'Hair) is the cosmic signature of the Seeker who must propitiate the White Goddess, through acceptance of her human representatives (women and the public generally) or her abstract countenance (the mystical, the irrational).

MERCURY-CHIRON

Along with Venus, Mercury has an approximately annual cycle, because it can never be located too far from Sol. The celestial Mercury-Chiron cycle refers to intellect, commerce, communication and coordination as elements of the Quest for self-transformation. In its initial phase, the conjunction of Mercury and Chiron, this cycle stands for an outpouring of mental energies with the objective of transmuting mundane activity into spiritual potential. Critical phases in this cycle, which correlate with the hard aspects between Mercury and Chiron (the square and opposition), represent crucial decisions initiated by the individual Seeker or forced on him/her by the demands of circumstances — these decisions (and the resulting actions) may be the result of a mentor's intervention. The soft aspects (sextile, trine and quincunx) generally represent information or communications received by the Seeker which have the effect of opening new doors or stimulating new ideas having to do with the process of self-transformation. It often happens that this new input is not recognized as significant until sometime after it is received.

With reference to the natal horoscope, the Mercury-Chiron cycle reveals the manner in which the individual uses his or her mental abilities (and this extends to the coordination of mind and body) in the service of the Quest. Specific phases in this cycle, represented by aspects, show how the native is most characteristically oriented to the use of mental abilities as a means for self-transformation. Mercury conjunct Chiron (as in the birth chart of Mormon patriarch Joseph Smith) signifies one who serves as a medium, a vehicle for the transmission of information aimed at other Seekers on the Path. Mercury sextile Chiron (present in the natal horoscopes of entertainers Goldie Hawn, Bette Midler and Linda Ronstadt, as well as politician Hubert Humphrey) indicates a facility for communication, a talent which is employed in the pursuit of the native's Quest. Mercury square Chiron (a factor in the birth charts of boxer Muhammad Ali, aviators John Glenn and Amelia Earhart, chess champion Bobby Fischer and journalist Clare Booth Luce) points to one whose mental abilities and/or mind/body coordination make possible key experiences which are conducive to the realization of self-transcendence — these experiences are often quite challenging, difficult or dangerous. Mercury trine Chiron (an aspect featured in the birth charts of Angela Davis and Anita Bryant) implies one whose Quest involves a position as a communicator, role model or teacher to some greater or lesser public. Mercury quincunx Chiron (exhibited in the natal charts of Mahatma Gandhi and Ann Morrow Lindbergh) suggests a Seeker who would be a servant, one who aims to take on the suffering of others by way of expiation — it is seldom a glamorous role, but it has its rewards as well as its penalties. And Mercury oppose Chiron (found in the birth charts of Jack Anderson, Meher Baba, Brigham Young and Maria Montessori) symbolizes one who seeks self-transformation through acting as a promoter, popularizer or guardian of whatever truth the Seeker regards as being revealed especially to him/her.

VENUS-CHIRON

The Venus-Chiron cycle, as mentioned in the previous section, is approximately annual in nature. This celestial cycle refers to magnetism, charisma, sexuality and grace, as well as other symbolically related matrices of experience (such as compassion, art, aesthetics, and social relationships in general). All these are initiatory rites of self-transformation under the aegis of the Venus-Chiron cycle. The conjunction of these two Planets marks the first phase in this process, signifying an intense concentration of Venusian qualities in preparation for the pursuit of the Quest. Hard aspects (the square and opposition) coincide with intense challenges, negative rewards of a social nature that force the Seeker to refine the seed of self-transcendence. Soft aspects (the sextile, trine and quincunx) signify an opportune phase in the cycle, a time when reward and outlets for expression are forthcoming if the Seeker is consciously attuned and emotionally receptive to their presence.

In terms of the natal horoscope, the Venus-Chiron cycle symbolizes the individual's potential for incorporating the Venus function as an element of the Quest. This function, which may be expressed through any of the experiential matrices associated with the Planet of Love, reaches a powerful intensity (albeit a generally unconscious intensity at first) with the conjunction of Venus and Chiron — an aspect found in the birth charts of Allesandro di Cagliostro, Evangeline Adams, Christine Jorgensen and Marilyn Monroe. (The latter two were born within two days of each other.) Venus sextile Chiron (found in the birth charts of Karl Marx, Abigail Van Buren, Anais Nin and Anita Bryant — the latter two having mutually opposing Chiron Signs, appropriately enough) denotes one whose Quest depends at least in part on influencing Venus functions in the social environment. Venus square Chiron (a factor in the natal horoscopes of Judy Garland and Karen Ann Quinlan) represents potential difficulties in the socialization process — these are challenges that serve as important learning experiences in the Quest for self-transformation. The trine between these two Planets promises an abundant opportunity for expressing the most altruistic end of the Venus spectrum: In this case (represented by the natal charts of Kurt Vonnegut, Albert Schweitzer and Mary Baker Eddy) there can be compassion and aesthetic vision in magnificent proportions. The Venus-Chiron quincunx (a factor in the birth chart of Gore Vidal) points to reserve (even secrecy) in the native's experience of such Venusian qualities as sexuality, sociability and the arts — this one's Quest is a delicate work of art in one sense or another. And finally, the Venus-Chiron opposition (present in the natal horoscopes of Aleister Crowley and Brigham Young) suggests a Seeker who has found a mentor, or who would be one for others — this individual must learn to handle an abundance of Venusian energies and experiences.

MARS-CHIRON

This cycle, approximately two years in length, is the first we have considered which entails a relationship between the Centaur Planet and one of the Superior Planets — the latter being defined as a Planet outside Earth's oribt. Superior Planet-to-Chiron cycles are longer in duration than those involving Chiron and the Sun, Moon, Mercury and Venus: This puts a special emphasis, a heightened symbolic significance, on Chiron's relationship to the Planets from Mars on outward.

The Mars-Chiron cycles refers to desire (the macho type, rather than the attractive Venus type of desire), aggression, courage, heroism and (paradoxically) healing — all of these functions being seen from the perspective of the transformative process. The cycle begins with the conjunction, symbolizing the outpouring of Martian energy in the service of some heroic Quest. Challenging peak points in the cycle coincide with hard aspects (the square and opposition), signifying intervals when adjustment and compromise must be made — or else conflict will result (the latter is generally the more likely). Soft aspects (the sextile, trine and quincunx) point to opportunities for channeling direct force to achieve a desired transformation, generally in cooperation with others: New information, new perspectives become available, revealing new avenues for action.

In the context of the natal horoscope, the Mars-Chiron cycle refers to the individual's potential for expressing Martian energy so as to achieve self-transformation. This potential is powerfully magnified under the aegis of the Mars-Chiron conjunction, which symbolizes a generally unconscious concentration of desire, force and courage in the native, who may use these qualities to attain the object of his or her Quest. (Natives of the Mars-Chiron conjunction include Argentine dictator Juan Peron, Ethiopian Emperor Haile Selassie, astrologer Sydney Omarr, athlete Wilma Rudolph, and actors Paul Newman and Robert Crane.) Mars sextile Chiron (a factor in the birth charts of Kurt Vonnegut, John Lennon and Amelia Earhart) indicates one whose strongest energies are channeled into the social/aesthetic sphere as a crucible of the Quest for self-transcendence. Mars square Chiron (found in the natal horoscopes of Aleister Crowley, Anne Frank, Jim Jones, Billie Jean King, Barry Goldwater, Timothy Leary and Jean Paul Sartre) denotes a seeker whose Quest must deal directly with issues of sexuality and aggression — to transform experiences of this nature into their healing analogs is an essential part of this individual's spiritual mission. Mars trine Chiron (exhibited in the natal charts of Jane Fonda, Judy Garland, Janis Joplin, Jack Kerouac, Karl Marx, Benjamin Spock, Carl Jung and Sigmund Freud) points to one whose charisma and/or special skills, augmented with considerable courage, are employed as a prime tool in the process of self-transformation. Marx quincunx Chiron (present in the birth charts of Marc Edmund Jones and Paramahansa Yogananda) indicates a Seeker who aims to perfect a technique requiring considerable discipline as a means to transcend the mundane limitations of selfhood. And finally, Mars oppose

Chiron (found in the natal horoscopes of Andrija Puharich and Abigail Van Buren) shows one who transmutes martial qualities into a healing force, thereby fulfilling an essential requisite of his or her individual Quest.

JUPITER-CHIRON

This cycle, which averages about fifteen years in duration, symbolizes a Quest of definite socio-cultural impact, although it of course does have purely personal correspondences as well. Optimism, enthusiasm, faith and abundance are keywords of the celestial interaction between Jupiter and Chiron. The cycle begins with the conjunction, which signifies an upwelling of hope and expectation channeled toward the realization of a transcendent objective. Critical points in the cycle coincide with the hard aspects (square and opposition), symbolizing conflict between the aims of a particular Quest and the limits imposed by the socio-cultural environment in which it operates. Especially opportune phases of the Jupiter-Chiron cycle coincide with the soft aspects (sextile, trine and quincunx), times when the socio-cultural environment is favorably disposed toward adopting (or at least tolerating) the aims and objectives of the Seeker and the Quest.

In the natal horoscope, the Jupiter-Chiron cycle indicates the individual's orientation toward harmonizing his or her Quest in relationship to the prevailing socio-cultural environment. The conjunction of these two Planets (present in the birth charts of nonviolent social reformer Martin Luther King, Jr., metaphysical astrologer Manly Palmer Hall, statistical astrology researcher Michel Gauquelin, cosmobiologist Reinhold Ebertin, and singers Edith Piaf, Frank Sinatra and Cher) symbolizes the hopeful, ebullient Seeker, the one whose Quest is marked by unfailing optimism in the pursuit of a desired transformation either of the self or the society — usually both. The sextile (found in the natal horoscopes of Christine Jorgensen, Marilyn Monroe, Muhammad Ali, Bishop James Pike, Bob Dylan, Richard Baba Ram Dass Alpert, Dr. Tom Dooley and the Reverend Jim Jones) portends one whose Quest meets with opportunities for social expression, often furnishing the Seeker with a forum for advancing his or her approach to self-transformation. The Jupiter-Chiron square (present in the natal horoscopes of Madame Blavatsky, Anita Bryant, Carlos Castaneda, Isadora Duncan, Madalyn Murray O'Hair and Abigail Van Buren) indicates one whose personal Quest tends to be at odds with prevailing socio-cultural norms at one point or another, giving rise to the possibility of more or less severe conflict. The trine (an element in the birth charts of Governor Edmund G. Brown, Jr., Meher Baba, Germaine Greer, Hubert Humphrey, Yoko Ono and Brigham Young) symbolizes the Seeker who aims to transform the socio-cultural environment in some way, given the opportunity — and it usually is given. The quincunx between these two Planets (a factor in the birth charts of Werner Erhard, Jane Fonda and John Glenn) signifies the Seeker whose Quest entails learning to handle interruptions and changes of direction with as much grace as possible. And finally, the opposition of Jupiter and Chiron (represented by the birth charts of Adolf Hitler, Carl Jung and Jack Kerouac) implies one whose Quest aims at a radical redirection of the socio-cultural environment — anarchy and occultism play a central role in this one's transformative vision.

SATURN-CHIRON

This is a long term cycle, with an average duration of approximately seventy-five years. There have been only two complete Saturn-Chiron cycles in the last two hundred years, one lasting sixty-four years and the other eighty-three years. This celestial cycle refers to socio-cultural restrictions on the Quest for self-transformation. It points to a resistance to transmutative energies, or to forces in the socio-cultural environment which aim to rigidly channel the transcendental impetus. The cycle begins with the conjunction of Saturn and Chiron, signifying an intensely crystallized will to achieve transmutation of personal and socio-cultural realities. Critical challenges to this impulse coincide with the hard aspects between these two Planets (the square and opposition), indicating challenging phases in the cycle, times when adjustment and compromise must be made, or else conflict will result — the latter is typically the more likely outcome, although each case must of course be considered on an individual basis. Opportunities arise coincident with the soft aspect phases of this cycle (the sextile, trine and quincunx), signifying times when constructive reform and appeals for discipline or restraint are apt to effect advances in personal and socio-cultural transformation.

With reference to the natal horoscope, the Saturn-Chiron cycle indicates limitations imposed upon the Seeker in pursuit of his or her Quest. These limitations may originate within the self, or they may have their origin in the socio-cultural environment. In any case they force the individual to steel himself/herself, to pass through a "dark night of the soul." The cycle begins with the Saturn-Chiron conjunction (a factor in the birth charts of Walt Whitman, Herman Melville, England's Prince Albert and Italian dictator Benito Mussolini), the hallmark of one whose Quest for self-transformation takes place in an environment of social rigidity, and proceeds only in the face of great difficulties and then only by virtue of an iron will. The sextile between these two Planets (present in the birth charts of Aleister Crowley, L. Ron Hubbard, Maharahj Ji and Albert Schweitzer) symbolizes one whose Quest involves the establishment of a socio-cultural legacy for the purpose of disseminating information on self-transformation. The square (present in the birth charts of Angela Davis, Uri Geller and Jane Fonda) points to a Seeker whose Quest entails conflict with particularly rigid elements of the socio-cultural environment — not an easy path to self-transcendence, but an effective one if pursued dauntlessly. The trine of Saturn and Chiron (represented in the birth charts of People's Temple founder Jim Jones and radium discoverer Marie Curie) symbolizes one whose Quest proceeds through long and painstaking labors, meeting with success in the same measure as the Seeker is able to maintain a strict regime of self-discipline. The quincunx (an aspect found in the birth chart of Carlos Castaneda) is the hallmark of one whose Quest is intensely secretive and dependent on strict discipline. And finally the opposition of Saturn and Chiron (present in the birth charts of columnist Jack Anderson, witch Sybil Leek and writer Kurt Vonnegut) signifies the Seeker whose path toward self-transformation leads to conflict with the socio-cultural environment: The Seeker must either compromise or face a bitter struggle as a consequence of pursuing his or her Quest.

CHIRON-URANUS

Because their orbital speeds are fairly closely matched, the Chiron-Uranus cycle is a long one, averaging more than one hundred and ten years in duration: In the last two hundred years, there has been only one complete cycle of these two Planets. This cosmic cycle refers to creativity and rebellion as elements in the pursuit of self-fulfillment and transmutation. It begins with the conjunction of Chiron and Uranus, signifying a mostly unconscious need for self-expression in new and revolutionary patterns. Critical phases in this cycle coincide with the hard aspects (square and opposition) of these two Planets, representing times when radically new (even desperate) forms of thought and behavior challenge the status quo. Soft aspects (the sextile, trine and quincunx) suggest intervals when offbeat, unconventional new directions are apt to meet with gradual acceptance despite an initial period of resistance.

In terms of the natal horoscope, the Chiron-Uranus cycle as a whole has little meaning for the individual as such. Alas, few of us now alive can expect to preserve our identities for one hundred and ten years or more. However everyone expresses the symbolic meaning of the Chiron-Uranus phase under which he or she is born — it stands for one's rebellious, idealistic, practicality-be-damned impulses as these relate to the Quest for self-transformation. The conjunction of these two Planets (exhibited in the birth charts of Ernest Hemingway, Alfred Hitchcock and Al Capone) suggests a Seeker whose Quest is more or less unconsciously motivated by a desire to be unique, daring and innovative. The sextile (present in the natal horoscopes of Meher Baba, Anita Bryant, Bob Dylan and Ringo Starr) points to one whose personal crusade for self-assertion and transcendence meets with opportunities in the social environment, giving rise to the potential for great influence over other Seekers. The Chiron-Uranus square (represented by the birth charts of Karl Marx and Friedrich Engels, Madame Blavatsky and Mary Baker Eddy; as well as George Harrison, Janis Joplin and the "boy guru" Maharaj Ji) symbolizes one whose pursuit of self-fulfillment and transformation is a difficult one, dogged by resistance from elements of the socio-cultural environment which regard the Seeker as anomalistic: There can be success with this aspect, to be sure, but it comes only through great struggle. The trine (illustrated by the natal horoscopes of Aleister Crowley, Goldie Hawn, Bette Midler, Linda Ronstadt and Albert Schweitzer) stands for the individual whose unique personal lifestyle is an expression of a Quest that attracts public notice either by accident or design, resulting in a social reaction which has a big influence on the Seeker — look for aspects to the personal Planets (Sun, Moon, Mercury and Venus) as signifiers of positive or negative public reation. The quincunx of Chiron and Uranus (present in Uri Geller's birth chart) points to one whose Quest is secretive or concealed, and depends on maintaining a strict regimen of personal discipline. And finally the opposition of Chiron and Uranus (illustrated by the birth charts of John Travolta and William "Buffalo Bill" Cody) symbolizes one whose personal Quest dramatizes individualism in its aspect as a defiance of social norms — a glorification of the "cowboy ethic", if you will.

CHIRON-NEPTUNE

With an average duration of approximately seventy-two years, this is another long-range Chiron cycle: Only two such cycles have been completed in the last two hundred years. The cycle begins with the conjunction of these two Planets, symbolizing an emotional or psychic intensity which finds expression through a Quest for transmutation. Critical phases in this cycle are signaled by the hard aspects (the square and opposition) of Chiron and Neptune, which point to emotional and psychic confrontation — in the absence of a sympathetic resolution, such confrontation can have a most trying effect on the drive toward self-transformation. Soft aspects (the sextile, trine and quincunx) between these two Planets stand for opportunities to express psychic or emotional energies in a way which is acceptable to the socio-cultural environment as well as conducive to the transformative process.

In the natal horoscope, the Chiron-Neptune cycle represents the individual's need to express psychic and emotional energies as a means toward the end of self-fulfillment and ultimate self-transcendence. The conjunction, first phase in this cycle (represented by the natal horoscopes of alchemist Allesandro di Cagliostro, writers Hermann Hesse ahd Upton Sinclair and dancer Isadora Duncan), points to a Seeker whose Quest is a mostly unconscious expression of powerful psychic and emotional energies — giving form to these energies serves this individual as a vehicle for self-transformation. The sextile (seen in the birth charts of Joan Baez, Bob Dylan, Jose Feliciano, John Lennon and Ringo Starr) symbolizes one whose Quest depends on the ability to communicate emotional images, dreams and poetic visions to others — for such a Seeker, isolation is sterility. The Chiron-Neptune square (present in the natal horoscopes of Karl Marx and Friedrich Engels, Mary Baker Eddy, Paramahansa Yogananda, Werner Erhard, Patricia Hearst and Karen Ann Quinlan) symbolizes one whose Quest must deal with such challenging Neptunian issues as spirituality, delusion, illusion and self-dissolution. The trine between these two Planets (exhibited in the birth charts of Annie Besant, Carlos Castaneda, Dr. Tom Dooley, Judy Garland, Martin Luther King, Jr., Sybil Leek and Kurt Vonnegut) stands for the Seeker whose Quest in regard to psychic, emotional and/or spiritual truth must ultimately take on a socio-cultural aspect — this one searches for the grail, so to speak, and exhorts others to do the same. The quincunx phase (represented by the birth charts of Jean Paul Sartre and Ann Morrow Lindbergh) is symbolic of the Seeker for whom self-transformation is an arduous, even evasive obligation, yet one which is rewarding in terms of spiritual satisfaction if pursued for its own sake, without hope or expectation of any other reward. And finally, the opposition of Chiron and Neptune (found in the birth charts of Enrico Fermi, Werner Heisenberg and Margaret Mead) points to one whose Quest is conducted in full knowledge of the fact that there are no facts — this one knows that only subjectivity is real, that objectivity is an illusion.

CHIRON-PLUTO

This cycle, approximately sixty years in duration on the average, has to do with mass currents of consciousness — the collective unconscious, the racial, cellular, molecular, atomic and subatomic levels of reality. The beginning of this cycle, heralded by the conjunction of Chiron and Pluto in the heavens, signals the upwelling of an initially unconscious impetus seeking expression as a historically necessary transmutation. Critical phases of the cycle, coinciding with the hard aspects between these two Planets (the square and opposition) augur resistance to the dialectic of mass transformation — there will be tension, there may be fierce conflict. Opportune phases equate with an easing of the tension between the status quo and the archetypal force which seeks to force its way into being.

In the context of the natal horoscope, the Chiron-Pluto cycle shows the individual's capacity to serve as a medium (a chalice or grail, if you will) for archetypal energies seeking to find concrete form in the human experience. The first phase of this cycle is the conjunction of Chiron and Pluto (an aspect found in the birth charts of Karl Marx and Friedrich Engels, as well as Joan Baez, Bob Dylan and John Lennon), which signifies a Seeker who may or may not be aware that his or her Quest for self-expression is the manifestation of a mass need, an instinct of the human spirit seeking an outlet at a particular time in history. The sextile phase (represented in the natal horoscopes of Richard Alpert, Anne Frank, Goldie Hawn, the Reverend Jim Jones, Yoko Ono, Linda Ronstadt and Barbara Walters) points to one whose self-transformation comes through having a finger on the mass pulse, and through being in some sense a reflection or spokesperson of that mass current of consciousness. The Chiron-Pluto square (seen in the birth charts of Betty Friedan, Sigmund Freud, Jack Kerouac, Timothy Leary, Sybil Leek, Paramahansa Yogananda and Kurt Vonnegut) symbolizes the Seeker who is conscious of the shape and direction of the archetypal urge: This one prepares the way, warns the unwary, and willingly takes on a Quest of struggle against the status quo in one way or another. Chiron trine Pluto (an aspect found in the natal horoscope of Nazi hunter Saul Wiesenthal, psychologist Rollo May, politician Barry Goldwater and alchemist Allesandro di Cagliostro) suggests one whose Quest is to express — through will, daring and strength of conviction — a mass yearning for integrity, for certainty based on inspiration. The Chiron-Pluto quincunx (found in the birth charts of Anais Nin and Patricia Hearst) represents a Seeker whose Quest must deal with such Plutonic issues as health, danger and sexuality. This one may be a puppet pulled by the strings of mass social movements, or one who manipulates the masses through an understanding of their innermost secrets. And finally, the opposition of these two Planets (a factor in the birth chart of Theosophist Annie Besant) points to a Seeker whose Quest is to embody, express and struggle on behalf of archetypal energies seeking to force their way into mass awareness.

CHAPTER 9

NOT THE LAST CHAPTER

This is the last chapter of this book, but it is not (I trust and hope) the last chapter in your discovery of Chiron. The archetypal functions symbolically associated with the Centaur Planet are too important to be picked up and then put down the way one handles a book. You have a Quest, a heroic labor of self-discovery, fulfillment and transcendence. You have had, now have and/or will have a mentor, a teacher whose presence inspires you and transforms your life. There is in you a healing, holistic impulse, a yearning to make your life whole, positive and complete, and to have the same transformative impact on everyone who touches your life. You have, either potentially or actually, the ability to synthesize dialectical opposites, to make sense of qualities and experiences that seem to struggle against each other in chaotic conflict. You are a bridge stretched over an abyss, a connection between eternity and mortality. All these and any other related ideas you can conceive pertain to Chiron. In a word, they refer to your Quest.

It is a grand and glorious notion, the Quest. Perhaps it seems anachronistic, out of synch with what we normally think of as human nature. If so, that is only because we fall too easily into the habit of mundane materialism. Chiron was discovered to remind us that we are more than the animal, more than "merely human." Like the Centaur, we are a union of the spiritual and the material. Just like Chiron, we are immortal beings born into a body where we experience countless joys and sufferings for a time — then at last we are returned to the heavens, the realm of archetypal energy.

There is no easy Quest, but perhaps the hardest of all is not to realize that you have a Quest. Ironically, that is the Path most human beings have chosen — if only because they have failed to choose anything else, failed to realize there is another possibility. You have a Quest, Dear Reader, whether you are aware of it or not.

Indeed, that is the metaphysical reason for Chiron's discovery. To make us aware, to provide for us an archetypal focus for self-transformation. Historically, the stage for this transmutative process was set with Charles Kowal's discovery of a Minor Planet in 1977. On a personal level, the rest is now up to you: Choose your Quest, begin the alchemical labor of transmutation.

In previous chapters we have examined some fundamental interpretations of Chiron's meaning in the natal horoscope, always with the injunction to understand what is written as a springboard for further personal exploration. The introduction is now completed, the rite of initiation has been prepared. Where your Quest takes you now is a matter far beyond my province as an astrologer. It is a matter to be decided between you and your Guide. As an author, I have written essentially all I have to say about Chiron and the Quest. The rest is for you to discover. At this point, the best I can do is to leave you with a shamanic rite, which in one form or another has served an untold number of Seekers well down through the ages. It is a way to go further than merely learning about your Guide and your Quest — it is a way to meet both on a personal (even transpersonal) level.

To begin, you must have the proper setting. Quiet and calm are essential. The setting must be conducive to meditation. The hypnagogic state, which is the stage preceding and following deep sleep, is the ideal place to personally encounter the Chiron archetype. Consequently it is advisable to begin your meditation while waiting to fall asleep. During this time, meditate on your natal horoscope, the map of your life potential. Think of Chiron's place in your chart, by House and Sign as well as by aspect. What does your Chiron Sign mean to you? How do you imagine Chiron's place (House) in your life? What is your Guide's relationship to the other forces and circumstances of your experience? Imagine your horoscope as the setting of a play, with the signs and houses as circumstances molding the actions of the Planets which occupy them. Pay special attention to Chiron's part in this drama.

As you find yourself slipping closer to the deep sleep stage, imagine yourself entering a cave. It is dark inside, and your eyes take a moment to adjust. At first you can see nothing at all, but gradually you make out the floor, walls and ceiling of the cave. Move through the cave, and as you proceed try to sharpen all your senses. You must strain to hear, strain to see, try your utmost to feel the inner walls and surfaces of the cave. You are as a stranger here, you are discovering a totally new environment. Get all your senses involved, until you feel fully at home in this new place. Now go deeper into the cave, exploring its vastness as you go. Be ready, be attentive — everything here is new to you, you don't know what you might find. Turn clockwise — always clockwise. If the cave branches out in two or more directions, always turn clockwise — to the right. Keep going, searching as you go. You are looking for any sign of movement in the darkness, any sound or other perception which might indicate that you are not alone. Keep searching — you will find what you are looking for. When you do, immediately get a handle on your perceptions at that instant. How do you feel about what you have seen, heard, or smelled? (The sense of smell is very important to you now.) What does it look like, how does it smell, what does it sound like? If you are at all uncomfortable, turn and go back the way you came at once. Do not be afraid, however — nothing can hurt you in here. It's just that anything which makes you uncomfortable is something or someone you are not yet ready to meet. Go back and try another time, but for the present just leave the cave.

There will come a time (it may take many visits to the cave) when you encounter a sign, something that points to a presence besides yourself, something that seems positive, accepting and inviting. This is the time, this is the sign for you. Go ahead at that point, move forward. What do you see? It may be an animal, a plant or a person, or it may be something else, perhaps a symbol with strong associations for you — a key for instance, or a bell, or perhaps a coin, in fact it could be anything at all that calls up a "Eureka!" feeling from within you. If it is a living thing, speak to it, ask it if it is your Guide, and then follow without reservation. If it answers yes, your search is of course over (more about that in a moment). Even if what you have found appears to be only an inanimate object, ask it if it is your Guide — you are in a magical dimension now, and anything is possible.

One way or another, you will find your Guide. Do not be surprised if the Guide you find bears little or no resemblance to the mythical image of Chiron the Centaur — Guides come in all forms, and they can change their appearance to suit (or to contrast with) your expectations. Your Guide may or may not look anything at all like what you expect, but if he or she (or it!) really is your Guide, you will be told so if only you ask. Some say the Guide is always a male figure — this is sexist nonsense. Some say the Guide is always human in appearance — this is hominid chauvinism. The only thing that is always true about your Guide is the feeling of complete loving trust and acceptance you will feel upon your first meeting — if this is not there, look elsewhere.

What happens next, once you have found your Guide? Of this I can say nothing, because every case is as unique as the individual involved. The important thing is what matters most to you. What troubles you? What isn't right in your life? Do you feel lost, unfilfilled? Whatever it is that counts most to you is the thing to ask your Guide about. Dialogue with your Guide. Do not hold back any question you may have. If you see your life in an astrological perspective, you may find it helpful to frame your questions in an astrological context. For instance if your health is a matter of immediate concern to you, ask your Guide about it. Ask the Guide to take you to your sixth house, your eighth house, your first house, etc. Ask to be led to Mercury — your Guide will take you anywhere, to meet anyone, even a god. Or if your love life isn't what you feel it should be, ask your Guide to take you to Venus, to the seventh house, the fifth house, to Mars, the Sun or the Moon. Whatever it is that makes you feel less than completely fulfilled, ask your Guide about it.

Do not expect your Guide to give you whatever you desire. The Guide's purpose is not to fulfill your every fantasy, but rather to show you how you must transform yourself in order to get where you want to be. Your Guide cannot solve your problems for you. However the Guide can help you realize just what the problem is (it's often quite different from what you might think at first), and how you can go about changing your life in order to make it better.

You may object, Dear Reader, that what is written here is only imagination. Do not let this stop you from trying it! In truth, everything is imagination, all is maya, there is nothing which is not an appearance. Readers with a background in psychology may prefer to think that the Guide meditation is merely an excursion into the subconscious. If that is what you prefer to believe, so be it. The important thing in any case is to try the meditation, or some variation on it: You will find your Guide. Your Quest is to find fulfillment, to transcend the limitations of human mortality. Your Guide, the Chiron function manifesting through you, will help you in your Quest. All you have to do is to seek, to ask, to dare.

Finally, a word of caution. I said earlier that there is nothing in the cave that can hurt you. This is absolutely and incontrovertibly true, if and only if you follow the instructions given above. In particular, remember to trust only the Guide who inspires a feeling of warmth, love and trust in you. And until you find such a Guide, avoid any other entities you may encounter in your meditation. There are gods in the cave, and there are demons too — some of the latter, as Aleister Crowley would say, will bite! Fear nothing and no one you may meet in the meditation, for fear gives power to dark forces. Should you come across anything unpleasant in the cave, bless it, turn around and walk (do not run!) back out the way you came. Having given you fair warning, I hereby wash my hands of any responsibility for anything that may happen if you fail to follow my injunction. As I say, have no fear — and have nothing whatsoever to do with anything in the cave that inspires any negative impression in you. All will be well.

APPENDIX I

CHIRON SIGN TABLE 1890-1999

01/01/1890 — 08/30/1890 — CAN	05/25/1926 — 10/20/1926 — TAU	03/27/1960 — 08/19/1960 — PIS
08/31/1890 — 02/14/1891 — LEO	10/21/1926 — 03/25/1927 — ARI	08/20/1960 — 01/20/1961 — AQU
02/15/1891 — 05/17/1891 — CAN	03/26/1927 — 06/06/1933 — TAU	01/21/1961 — 03/31/1968 — PIS
05/18/1891 — 10/11/1891 — LEO	06/07/1933 — 12/22/1933 — GEM	04/01/1968 — 10/18/1968 — ARI
10/12/1891 — 03/01/1893 — VIR	12/23/1933 — 03/23/1934 — TAU	10/19/1968 — 01/30/1969 — PIS
03/02/1893 — 06/18/1893 — LEO	03/24/1934 — 08/28/1937 — GEM	01/31/1969 — 05/28/1976 — ARI
06/19/1893 — 10/10/1894 — VIR	08/29/1937 — 11/23/1937 — CAN	05/29/1976 — 10/13/1976 — TAU
10/11/1894 — 10/07/1896 — LIB	11/24/1937 — 05/28/1938 — GEM	10/14/1976 — 03/28/1977 — ARI
10/08/1896 — 10/29/1898 — SCO	05/29/1938 — 09/30/1940 — CAN	03/29/1977 — 06/19/1983 — TAU
10/30/1898 — 01/12/1901 — SAG	10/01/1940 — 12/31/1940 — LEO	06/20/1983 — 11/29/1983 — GEM
01/13/1901 — 08/09/1901 — CAP	01/01/1941 — 06/17/1941 — CAN	11/30/1983 — 04/11/1984 — TAU
08/10/1901 — 09/29/1901 — SAG	06/18/1941 — 07/27/1943 — LEO	04/12/1984 — 06/21/1988 — GEM
09/30/1901 — 04/22/1904 — CAP	07/28/1943 — 11/18/1944 — VIR	06/22/1988 — 07/21/1991 — CAN
04/23/1904 — 05/21/1904 — AQU	11/19/1944 — 03/24/1945 — LIB	07/22/1991 — 09/04/1993 — LEO
05/22/1904 — 01/11/1905 — CAP	03/25/1945 — 07/22/1945 — VIR	09/05/1993 — 09/08/1995 — VIR
01/12/1905 — 03/19/1910 — AQU	07/23/1945 — 11/10/1946 — LIB	09/09/1995 — 12/29/1996 — LIB
03/20/1910 — 08/29/1910 — PIS	11/11/1946 — 11/28/1948 — SCO	12/30/1996 — 04/05/1997 — SCO
08/30/1910 — 01/15/1911 — AQU	11/29/1948 — 02/09/1951 — SAG	04/06/1997 — 09/03/1997 — LIB
01/16/1911 — 03/31/1918 — PIS	02/10/1951 — 06/18/1951 — CAP	09/04/1997 — 01/07/1999 — SCO
04/01/1918 — 10/22/1918 — ARI	06/19/1951 — 11/04/1951 — SAG	01/08/1999 — 06/01/1999 — SAG
10/23/1918 — 01/28/1919 — PIS	11/05/1951 — 01/28/1955 — CAP	06/02/1999 — 09/22/1999 — SCO
01/29/1919 — 05/24/1926 — ARI	01/29/1955 — 03/26/1960 — AQU	09/23/1999 — 12/31/1999 — SAG

APPENDIX II

HOW TO GET YOUR CHIRON HOROSCOPE

The easiest way to get your Chiron birth chart is to have it done by Astro Computing Services (P.O. Box 16430, San Diego, CA 92116), a leader in computerized horoscope calculation. It will cost you just two dollars for the chart itself, plus a one dollar handling charge per order. The service is fast, too — your order will be processed the day it arrives. Here's all you have to do:

First, ascertain the exact time, date and place of your birth. Accuracy is crucial. If at all possible, obtain a copy of your full birth certificate. You may need to write the Vital Statistics Office in the state of your birth, asking for a certified copy of your full birth certificate (not the short form!), making special mention of the fact that you want to know the time of your birth. Generally this costs just a few dollars, and as a rule you'll need to provide the following information: Your full legal name as well as your parents' full legal names (including your mother's maiden name); also your sex and race, and the month, day and year of your birth; and finally your birthplace; (city or town, county or parish, state and name of hospital if any). If it is absolutely impossible to get a copy of your full birth record, try digging through your family archives — a family bible, your baby book, etc. Should this prove a dead-end route, you might try asking your parents what time you were born — this is a next-to-last resort, however, to be used only if just about everything else fails. If for whatever reason none of the above options will work for you, contact a reputable astrologer in your area and ask to have your birth date determined through chart rectification — desperate circumstances call for desperate measures!

Once you have your full birth data, send this information along with a check or money order in the amount of three dollars to Astro Computing Services. Be sure to include your return address! Specify that you want your natal horoscope *with Chiron included*! (If you do not specifically mention that you want a chart complete with Chiron, you won't get it.) Please bear in mind that what you will get is essentially just a natal horoscope (albeit with Chiron included), plus some technical data such as aspects, planetary nodes, declinations, etc. What you will not get is a text, an interpretation of the chart in so many words. You can use the delineations provided in this book to get you started in interpreting Chiron's place in your natal horoscope, and there are a number of astrology primers listed in Appendix III to help you interpret the rest of the chart.

APPENDIX III
SELECTED BIBLIOGRAPHY

ASTROLOGY PRIMERS (with instructions on horoscope calculation)

Marion March and Joan McEvers, *The Only Way to Learn Astrology*, Vols. I-III. San Diego, CA: Astro Computing Services, 1981-1982.

Michael R. Meyer, *A Handbook for the Humanistic Astrologer.* Garden City, NY: Doubleday/Anchor, 1974.

REFERENCES

Malcolm Dean, ed., *Ephemeris of Chiron*, 2nd Revised Edition. Toronto, Canada. Phenomena Publications, 1982.

Nicholas DeVore, *Encyclopedia of Astrology.* New York: Philosophical Library, 1947.

Neil F. Michelsen, *The American Atlas.* San Diego, CA: Astro Computing Services, 1978.

-----, *The American Book of Tables.* Astro Computing Services, 1976.

-----, *The American Ephemeris for the 20th Century.* Astro Computing Services, 1980.

Marc Penfield, *2001: The Penfield Collection.* Seattle, WA: Vulcan Books, 1979.

Lois M. Rodden, *The American Book of Charts.* Astro Computing Services, 1980.

-----, *Profiles of Women.* Tempe, AZ: American Federation of Astrologers, 1979.

Helen Weaver, et. al., *Larousse Encyclopedia of Astrology.* New York: McGraw-Hill, 1980.

GENERAL

Isaac Asimov, *Saturn and Beyond*. New York: Lothrop, Less and Shepard Co., 1979.

Robert Graves, *The Greek Myths*. New York: Braziller, 1959.

-----, *The White Goddess*. New York: Noonday Press, 1966.

Robert Hand, *Horoscope Symbols*. Rockport, MA: Para Research, Inc., 1981.

Charles Kingsley, *The Heroes*. New York: Schocken Books, 1970.

Erminie Lantero, *The Continuing Discovery of Chiron*. York Beach, ME: Samuel Weiser, Inc. (forthcoming).

Dane Rudhyar, *The Astrology of Personality*. Garden City, NY: Doubleday, 1970.

-----, *The Astrology of Transformation*. Wheaton, IL: Theosophical Publishing House, 1980.

Edwin C. Steinbrecher, *The Inner Guide Meditation*. Santa Fe, NM: Blue Feather Press, 1978.

Noel Tyl, *Holistic Astrology*. McLean, VA: TAI Books, 1980.

John Updike, *The Centaur*. Greenwich, CT: Fawcett Crest Books, 1967.

PERIODICALS

Aquarian Changes, Journal of D.O.M.E. Inner Guide Meditation Center: P.O. Box 1159, Boulder, CO 80306.

The Key, Newsletter of the Association for Studying Chiron: 757 E. Main St., K201, Lansdale, PA 19446.